Motherwell

A Walk Down Memory Lane

The Bridge Over the Thames At Motherwell

With Jack L Cooke

©2007,2009 Jack L. Cooke

ISBN: 978-0-9808983-3-0

Permission to reproduce in any form must first be secured from
Jack L Cooke, 735 Deveron Crescent, London, Ontario N5Z 4X8
E mail – jlcooke@sympatico.ca

Also by Jack L Cooke:
Getting By In A Silent World
The Life and Times Of Jack L Cooke
Published 2005
Reprinted 2009

The History Press
94 Lillian Crescent,
Barrie, ON L4N 5H7
Tel: (705) 728-5802 Fax: (705) 728-0048
www.thehistorypress.ca
publishing@thehistorypress.ca

Contents

A Walk Down Memory Lane 7

They Came To A New Land 13

Living With Grandpa And Grandma 21

When I Was A Boy In The 30's... 25

A Walk In The Woods 31

The Wood Cutting Bee 39

The Love Of Old Barns... 45

Billy Our Farm Goat 51

Grandpa's Red Durham Cows 59

My Grandpa's Orchard 67

Profound Deafness 73

Taking Uncle Guy Fishing.. 79

The Barn Swallow... 85

Pete Our Feathered Friend 91

Where Did All The Aprons Go 97

The Barn Sparrow 103

The Starling...109

When Credit Was Your Good Name 115

The Hired Man 119

The River 125

My Dad's Cars 135

Finding Happiness 151

FOREWORD

Well Jack my boy, you've done it again. Having published your first book, "Getting by in a Silent World", where you showed us all that you have been able to accomplish, even though you are unable to hear, now you have put your memory to work and told us all about what it was really like growing up during the 30's and 40's in Rural Ontario.

It has been a privilege to have had an opportunity to play some part in helping you complete these most interesting stories about your early life. I wonder how many of us, gentle readers, are smug in the belief that we know all there is to know about our past because we have studied from those history books in school. History books are valuable, but they don't get right into the detailed stories about what life was really like.

This easy-to-read book blows away the cobwebs and lets us look through the windows into farming life as it was when farmers were shaping the history of the province of Ontario. The short stories, of which this book is comprised, means that one can sit down and read one story at a time, then leave it for a while and return without missing where you left off. (but I bet you will not be able to put it down)

This book will bring back memories for some and inform others while preserving the best of our rural heritage. Have a Happy Read

Ralph Smith

Old Farm Water Wells 157

Monday Is Wash Day..165

The Mailman..171

Winter And Snow 177

Linda And My Tulips..183

The Tulip Extravaganza..189

Our Ever Changing World..195

The Field Of Dreams And The Shadows Of War................................203

Mixed Farming As I Remember It...215

Memories Of Christmas Past 221

Soft Water 227

Wake Up And Smell The Coffee 233

A Family That Eats Together..237

A Wondrous Gift..243

My Dad And The Butcher Knife 247

Home-Made Bread..251

Memories Of Other Times..257

TIP – To Insure Promptness 265

One Cold Winters Day In St. Marys...273

The First TV Set in 1951 279

Dad And His Toys 283

The Country Garden 295

Will You Remember Me Jack-A 301

4

Preface

Recently while working on my Family Tree I uncovered a new appreciation for our heritage and the history of the Township of Fullarton and the village of Motherwell, Ontario. I have always been proud to carry the family name Cooke and to say, "I came from Motherwell". For me it is where life began, and every now and then I return to the village, to the river and the old farm to evaluate my thoughts. Once upon a time -- for me, it was the center of the earth.

We came from a humble lineage of English and Scottish farmers and tradesmen. Very early in our lives we were taught that our pioneer forefathers were very hard working, honest and honorable folks and it was our duty to preserve the things they taught us --- their ways, their good name and above all the trust we have in one another.

<u>Motherwell</u> -

Today the village of Motherwell is in despair, a shadow of its past. There was a time when it was the very heart of life within the community. A place where the locals gathered at the general store, sharing fond greetings and exchanging news and views while buying basic groceries for their family. God brought our pioneer forefathers to this great country and made it possible for us to live together in decency, in truth, in honesty.

These elements are among the basic instincts of our nature. They are with us always. If we were to depart from them we would defeat ourselves and throw away the possibility of our highest achievements, fulfillments and blessings

This leads me to say that while we have a great heritage in our community, a lasting mutual respect and love for one another we have an even greater heritage in the fact that as a community we were blessed as we grew up within the church; thus we belong to the family of God. Now in our later years it comforts us and gives us peace.

In my book, "A Walk Down Memory Lane" I wish to show honour and respect for all the good things in that past, as I have known it.

A Walk Down Memory Lane

8

A Walk Down Memory Lane

Once Upon A Time

Fifty years and more have passed since I left the farm and now when I venture onto one I feel like a stranger. I am lost amid towering machines and storage bins and strange looking Quonset buildings, pole barns and unfamiliar cash crops. Everything is done now on a gigantic scale. All those ten-acre fields have long disappeared along with the fence posts. The old bank barns are gone or are far apart. Many farms have no fences at all or only a line fence. There used to be a well-known old saying. "Good fences make good neighbours".

At one time I was sure I knew everything there was to know about farming. Most farm enterprises at that time were referred to as Mixed Farming, which means farming a wide variety of things from chickens to hogs and most likely along with either beef or dairy cattle. There might be a field of cash crop grain. Every year you made a few dollars from your bush by selling maple syrup, and every few years you sold a few logs to the local saw mill.

When I left the farm teams of old horses were still grazing the pasture fields. True, they were getting old but they led a pampered life and looked fat and sleek. Who could picture any farm without a team of horses? Every now and then when the farmer went near them they perked their ears and lifted their heads knowingly, perhaps even hopefully that they might be of some use.
They too had memories of a time when they were worth their oats. Perhaps in their great hearts they knew their years were numbered. Their last few years were easy ones as many farmers felt they belonged to the farm and had earned their keep.

In Fullarton Township and Perth County we no doubt inherited many aspects of this kind of farming from our mother countries of England, Scotland, Ireland, France and Germany. However I do believe the nature of Ontario's climate and landscape at that time had a lot to do with the way we farmed.

On the other hand there is no doubt in my mind but that we were enslaved by the very system we had invented. This deeply imbedded idea of a safety net of several types of farming kept us on the run 7 days a week every week of the year

In my lifetime I have worked at many things. Some of those things were not the kind of jobs I wanted to do for a lifetime, but on the other hand some of those jobs taught me a new respect for those who laboured. Some of those jobs showed me the kind of stuff I was made of. Few suffered long from a bout of hard work

Still there were many people with a deep affection, yes, even a love for farming and the commitment to the land they worked. It was to them not so much a job as a way of life. The satisfaction they got from doing the job, and doing it well, was more than equal to the cost - be it dollars from their pocket or years from their lives.

Farmers at that time seldom acknowledged great satisfaction in the wealth of dollars earned, but rather the satisfaction of doing well, and getting the job done.

My fondest memories are of that picture-perfect mixed farm while I am sitting still under a warm sun on a Sunday morning. Everything around me for a short time has come to a comfortable halt. Yet nothing has been left undone. The great wheat straw stack sits proudly in the middle of the barnyard and the milk cows lie contentedly about munching on the newly threshed straw that covers the yard. The hens are also checking it out burying themselves up to their necks in fresh clean straw in hopes of finding the odd kernel of wheat. My view reflected our wealth.

Now that the crop is off you can see all the way back over the farm to the bush.
On either side of the lane are neat looking ten-acre fields of golden stubble one after the other all the way to the rear of the farm.

The farmer knows the true meaning of the word harvest. He planted his seed and worked towards it all year. He has earned it with sweat and labour. He knows there is a deep and profound satisfaction that does not come to anyone who just earns a paycheck. He is very aware that this harvest is a gift, thus he is humbled and thankful to the Lord.

Yes, things have changed down on the farm and it may be much more rewarding and perhaps a lot less hard work. However to me it has lost that tranquil setting that endeared it to so many generations of Canadians.
In my minds eye I still see it, as it was, "Once Upon A Time."

The big brick house with its many gable ends, the great bank barn on its field stone wall and the towering maples in the lane, and an orchard full of trees. I see cows and calves and horses in the field and chickens in the yard.

Perhaps my book will remind you of the good and the bad, of how it used to be.

It is to you my dear friends and to my sisters and families I dedicate this book, for the many ways you have touched my life. Enjoy and God Bless.

Morning Mist On The Old Farm Over My Dad's Corn Field

They Came To

A

New Land

14

They Came To A New Land

With Hope and A Prayer

Napoleon surrendered to Britain on July 15th 1815 after the battle of Waterloo. The English and Scottish soldiers returned home and could not find jobs. The war had created an industrial revolution in both England and Scotland. This was nowhere more evident than for the weavers in the factories in Northern England and Southern Scotland. They had lost their jobs to a machine that could do the work of many men and do it longer, better and cheaper.

The unemployment in both England and Scotland was troublesome. The weavers and small shop owners, the crop-sharers and tenant farmers pawned all of their belongings and then went on government assistance. The wealthy were burdened with more and more taxes to keep the poor and the many that were unemployed. The rich thought the answer to this problem was to hire boats and send the poor and unemployed off to the new colony of Canada. Thus started the great emigration from England and Scotland and Ireland to Canada. They came by the tens of thousands and few had any regrets.

The Arrival of New Canadians

When the settlers arrived they were warmly greeted. Each family was provided with what were thought the necessities of life at that time. They received 5 blankets. 1 axe, 1 pick axe, 1 spade, 1 saw, 1 hammer, 2 hoes, 1 reap hook, 1 kettle, 1 wedge, 1 file, a pair of hinges, a lock and key.

Money was also to be provided, to be given to them in 3 installments over the next 6 months. Each was given 100 acres of land without a deed until they repaid their debt. They thought they were in heaven. It was all given to them with trust and the understanding it was to be repaid in ten years.

There were a lot of good intentions both by the government and these new settlers. However they were taken out into solid bush country of Lanark County in Eastern Ontario and turned loose. They were shocked to find such a forest of huge maple, beech and elm trees on their land. Many of these people knew very little about farming and much less about logging or cutting down huge trees to clear land. However together they set about building log houses and clearing land.

Then Ten Years Later

Ten years later they had built their homes and cleared some land and built a small community. However they had little to show in the line of cash to pay back the government loan. The government would not give them the deed to their land until the loan was repaid. So many walked off and left everything behind as they had heard rumors of better land to the west in what was called the Huron Tract.

In 1833 the government hired a surveyor to study the quality of the area and the living condition of these settlers. He determined that the land was unfit for farming as some areas were too rocky and other areas were swampland. He determined the settlers too poor to pay the debt. In 1837 the government cancelled the debt and issued the deed to them for the land.

The New Land And Paradise Found

Of course some farmers on the best land stayed on in Lanark County but many had heard of this new trail called the Huron Road being cut through a virgin territory called The Huron Tract. This trail was to open the land all the way from York (Toronto) and Guelph to Goderich on the great lake, Lake Huron.

The land was advertised to be very free of stone and the soil very rich. In its very heart was a township called Fullarton with a gentle river called the Thames flowing right down its very centre from north to south.

Many settlers arrived by boat at Hamilton and then travelled by stagecoach or by wagon to Guelph then followed the new trail, The Big Road as they called it, west.

Because of the earlier settlement in eastern Ontario there were many young first generation Canadian children born in Canada among the new settlers. These children would prove to be a wonderful advantage to them in time on this new adventure, as many hands were needed to clear this new land. They eventually arrived in Mitchell, a village on the north branch of the Thames River. In 1836 the Canada Company had laid out the town plots along the Huron Road

The weary travelers would find a place to stay at the newly erected log hotel-tavern erected for Canada Company by John Hicks. It was built near the banks of the Thames River on the Logan side of the Huron Road.

Once they had rested they followed the river south to a village called Fullarton. There they found English and Scottish settlers who had already settled the land close to the river so they chose a place a few miles farther south down the river.

The Bryce Skinner Log House On The Mitchell Road

A Place Called Motherwell

They arrived at their chosen destination. The river ambled close against its west side bank and there were broad river flats to the east. This was a perfect site for a village surrounded by rolling land that was self-drained to the river, so they settled there. They called the village Motherwell after the village of Motherwell in Scotland.

For so many of us this is the place where it all began. This is the place we will forever look back on and call home. --- Motherwell

Stone Houses Along The Thames River At Motherwell

The Harvey & Janette Roger House

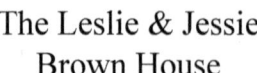

The Leslie & Jessie Brown House

The John and Reta
Cooke Second Home
on the Thames

The George & Sadie
Cooke House

The
George Parker House

The Field Stone Home of Prime
Minister Arthur Meighen

Living With Grandpa and Grandma

Living With Grandpa and Grandma

After my dad and mom were married my Grandpa and Grandma lived in a small part of the old farmhouse. There was a very small kitchen with one window that looked out into the orchard. There was also a "front parlour" as it was called, furnished with what I thought was ancient furniture. The furniture was always kept under cover with dust throws until company came. In the center of the ceiling was a beautiful plaster molding of many kinds of fruits. There were grapes with beautiful leaves and oranges and apples and many other things. In the very center of it was a hook, and hanging from the hook was a coal-oil lamp that pulled down on a chain. We seldom saw it lit but when it was the room glowed with a soft mellow enchanting light. Of course it was saved for special company.

Then there was also a bedroom with a long narrow closet that stretched out far back under the front hall staircase. The bedroom had a window that looked out onto the back open deck of the summer kitchen, so as a rule the blind was drawn and curtains pulled. All this was small but cozy and always much warmer than the rest of the huge old house.

The Old Cooke Farm House

It seemed as children we felt free to walk in unannounced on my grandparents at any time. Sometimes we even announced that we were going to put on a program for them that evening. I don't remember ever feeling we were intruding and we were never told to go home. It seemed they were always happy to have us visit, and that was several times every day from all four of us. There must be a special reward for grandparents up there in heaven.

My grandfather would sit in his armchair in the corner of their small kitchen and whittle wood. He made tops that spin and whistles and even amazing dancing dolls. I often crawled up on his knee and he told me many stories of a mighty and glorious place called England. I listened with awe and respect. I knew nothing of the world beyond our community. To me it was the center of the world.

My world at that time was very small. For the most it circled around the farm itself. In time it would include the huge red brick school on the road to the village of Motherwell and most certainly the old white brick United Church with the towering columns on the Mitchell road. Both will always be a part of me.

The Motherwell United (Presbyterian) Church

A rare treat was to get off the farm and go to the village store at Motherwell along with my dad. I loved the sound of the jingle of the bell over the door when we entered and the smell of the dry goods stacked all around me within the store.

Upon returning home I got to deliver grandpa's tobacco and grandma's groceries to their kitchen. As a rule there was always a just reward.

I was growing up ever so slowly, trying to understand about life in the 1930's.

When I Was

A Boy In The

30's

When I Was A Boy In The 1930's

There was a time in my life when it seemed all things around me stood still. It was as if all this had been there forever and nothing ever changed.

My grandparents lived in one part of the huge brick house. I saw them everyday and loved them dearly. It seemed as if they had always been there.

The house I lived in,
The big old silver grey bank barn,
Standing high and proud on its
fieldstone walls
It too had always been there.

The farmland as a whole,
The bush and swamp,
The land my father tilled,
This too had always been there

Keith Watson, Bert Dow, Ralph Smith. Bruce Roger,. Jack Cooke. Earl Roger, Ken Dow, Stanley Morrison Jack Watson

My dad had a herd of milk cows. I knew them by name. There were calves and yearlings and a number of pigs from old sows to fat hogs and the flock of red hens that belonged to my mom. To me this too, had always been. I suppose one might look at this way of life as giving a child the feelings of security, a home and a place of refuge.

Life as I remembered it from day to day may have registered a lot of hard work but within it was a kind of sanctuary, a feeling of being safe and secure. We knew we were poor but we never went hungry. Our shoes may have been worn and our everyday clothes tattered but our neighbours looked just the same so it didn't seem to matter.

This feeling of security may have come from the way we lived. It was both good and bad as while it kept us safe from harm on bad years it also kept us from making a good profit on the good years. In other words if you're smart you followed the crowd and never put all your eggs in one basket. Everyone was taught from a little child up that change was not a smart move so in your life you never take a chance. Play it safe.

My grandfather and my dad had known both good and hard times, and they had suffered great loss so now they never took any chances. I think it was the mind-set of mixed farming at that time that tended to do that to people. At the expense of long hours and hard work in our daily lives old-fashioned mix farming added stability to farming but seldom any great wealth.

Then too, our community itself was a balanced mixture of people, young to old. Old people were all around us. They were loved and cared for. No one ever called them by their first names out of respect. Our next-door neighbours were Mr. and Mrs. Roger and next to them was Mr. Morrison and down the road there was Mr. and Mrs. Bar. No one who was anyone had to go off to a place they called an "Old People's Home." Like my grandpa and my grandma they died at home in their own bed. All this was unwritten security.

In our community the old folks lived in one part of the family home. They looked after the children when the mother went outside to work in the garden or to feed the chickens and hens or help with the milking. To me it seemed quite natural for my grandparents to do this for us as they belonged to us and we to them, and after all, they had always been there.

They had always been old and I had always been young. Nothing ever changed.

Eventually though it seems time did move on almost unnoticed by me. The brick on the old farmhouse changed its colour to a darker cream and the wide hemlock boards on the barn weathered and mellowed and turned to a softer hue of silver grey. The most tragic change though for me was the loss of my Grandpa Cooke. He passed away from cancer April 21, 1941 when I was 12 years old.

In those awkward years of 13 and 14, I only saw the drabness side of farm life. I think most or perhaps all boys go through a stage of life when they are trying to leave childhood behind yet not quite ready to grow up. Being an only boy on a farm far out in the country and not feeling close to my dad didn't help.

At 14, I had scarlet fever and was in danger of losing my hearing. Perhaps for the first time I was more concerned about the future instead of pondering the past.

When I was 15 years old and coming 16 the fall of 1944 I left home for Western Canada. I fell in love with the west and its people. I guess you might say I was at the age of enlightenment and felt the need of a great escapade. I absorbed all the things around me. I was never more happy or felt more alive. When I came back home I saw things differently. Where I used to see drabness I now saw beauty. Life came to me and even though my hearing was getting worse I felt more able to cope.

One might say that a year of growth away from home had brought on a new awakening within me and perhaps I needed this in my search for change.

The old folks all around me one by one had passed away. I had looked at them as timeless. Having them among us made us feel loved. They gave us the feeling of worth. Honesty, respect, love and genuine care shone from their faces and ebbed from their presence. All these things of great importance in life now in their old age they seemed to have in abundance. I realize now that time does change things, and perhaps there comes a time when we all have to move on.

Moving on though meant taking a chance. I am not sure I ever really wanted to farm but it was home and I felt as if I belonged. My dad though made it clear to me very early in life, I was not going to get the farm. I wasted a lot of time trying to find a steady job but as soon as they found out I permeate hearing problem they politely put me off.

I knew the total loss of my hearing was inevitable; it was just a matter of time. Somehow I must prepare myself for it. My mind though was not ready for this. I willed everything to stay the same. The only security I had ever known was that of my grandfather and to the old farm. I knee I would do whatever it took to find that security. However the good Lord too had a plan for me and it meant I had to make a change. That change for me was very challenging as it meant giving up the farm to move to the city. Things turned out well for me in the end

On the other hand over the years mixed farming slowly changed … and the farmer too found out sometimes change is good.

The Boy Mother Thinks You Are

While walking through a crowded town street the other day
I heard a little urchin to his comrade turn to say
"Say Jimmy let me tell youse I'd be happy as a clam
If I was de feller dat me mudder thinks I am.
Gee Jim she t'inks dat I'm a wonder and she know her little lad
Auld never mix wid nothin' dat was ugly, mean or bad.
Lots er times I sits and t'inks how nice t'would be, gee whiz
If a feller only was de feller his mudder t'inks he is."
My friend be yours a life of toil or undiluted joy,
You still can lean a lesson from this small unlettered boy
Don't aim to be an earthly saint with your eyes fixed on a star
Just try to be the fellow that your mother thinks you are   Edgar Guest

Once Upon A Time With My Friend Bill Stephens

Bill still keeps a team of horses around today

A Walk in the Woods

A Walk In The Woods

    I always feel I am a better person because of my rural roots. While I believe I adapted to city life very well I have never been shy about my country behavior. Thus at times I confuse my city friends with my thoughts and my rustic ways. There is an old saying that you can take the boy out of the country but you can't take the country out of the boy. After all of these years I know it is true.

    At times they say, "Were you born in the bush"? Not so much to ask, as to inform me.

    I sometimes think it is really true, just maybe I <u>was</u> born in the bush, and it's strange, as it doesn't bother me a bit.

    You see our old farm on the Mitchell Road, north of the village of Motherwell Ontario was surrounded by bush. There were two solid bush farms to the north side of the home farm stretching from the Mitchell Road all the way to the back end. Then bush again all across the back end even encroaching on the back field on the south side of our 100 acres. Then there were our 62 1/2 acres next door to the south that my grandfather was trying to clear. It was a mixture of swamp at the rear and bush coming far up the south side of the home farm. It also had a gravel pit and a water pond. It was a place of great interest to a small boy as I liked to venture deep into the willow swamp and sometime I would swim nude in the water hole with many great green frogs for company.

Across the road from the house and barn was the bush at the rear end of my dad's brother's place, my Uncle George's farm. His house and barns were on the River Road high on the banks of the Thames.

All along the road at the front of the farm were great old soft maple trees reaching high into the sky. There were tall maples in the lane on the one side and tall spruce on the other. To add to all this there was my grandfather's orchard. Yes, no doubt about it I was born in the bush and every now and then I get the urge to go back, perhaps hoping to recapture a time, a place in the past but I fear it is lost as nothing is ever quite the same.

In the evening or early morning the deer came from the bush to browse on the fields of grain, and on cold winter nights they came to the orchard along with cottontails and jackrabbits to munch on the apples left on the ground.

At other times the ring-neck pheasants came to the orchard or to the barnyard along with pesky squirrels. Yes it's true, it was almost as if I was born and brought up in the bush, as it seemed we were surrounded by nature, the animals and the birds, the bush and swamp. I have very pleasant thoughts of that part of my life.

Having the bush so close to you fills you with the urge to explore. It's all very well to have those furry and feathered friends from the bush come to visit you, but you're filled with the desire to go to them. While your furry friends and feathered friends may come to you for food for their tummy, I found out I went to the bush for food for the soul.

When spring came it seemed my sister Pearl and I would sneak off to the bush to explore. When we started out walking along with Toby our old farm dog we had no intention of going quite so far, but eventually we would be deep into the swamp on the sixty and at times even lost. It was just one of those things that happened in the spring every year.

After being missing for a few hours we knew there would be punishment when we did turn up at home but that didn't hurry us along one bit.

After many years it seemed my mother got to expect it and she would say to the neighbour, "Well It must be spring, Jack and Pearl disappeared to the bush."

I like to remember the year I was boiling sap in our bush in Uncle Hugh's pan. The steam was rolling off the pan into the chilly spring air. The team of horses Barney and Slim were standing patiently on the side enjoying the feeling of nature at its best all about them. The breeze was just a bit more than what I would call comfortable, but the heat coming from the fireplace kept me warm.

There are times when you can feel the stillness

While my hearing was fast leaving me I still had some left. Sometimes it seemed better than others. From afar I heard the wondrous sound of an organ coming to me through the tree tops. It came to me in waves as the wind blew through the trees. At first I could not believe what I was hearing as it truly did sound so real and heavenly at times up close and at other times far, far away. It would rise into a high crescendo and then fall back to a low hum, mysterious, wonderful, and beautiful … all of that. I am told others have heard it too. It is explained that when many tree branches rub or saw together, it has the same effect that a bow has on a violin. Everyone should experience it at least once in a lifetime. It's as if God and nature were working in harmony in its wondrous ways.

Such an experience led me to feel that I could find solace in a walk in the woods. As a boy growing up alone on the farm, I found I needed to take many of those walks alone in the woods. Like all boys and young men I had my share of trouble sorting out life's problems. Being alone without a brother didn't help.

When I went for a walk in the woods what I found was a kind of spiritual abidance, a place of order. I could feel it as it was all about me. Not a physical presence but a feeling of consciousness, like that of entering a great church, and it brought me closer to God, thus solving many of my problems.

When There Is No Clear Path To Follow

I believe there are times in all people's lives when life may seem confusing and there seems to be no clear path for us to follow. Trust me, go for a walk alone in the woods and you will feel a stillness that enters and quiets your soul. As I walked I would feel His presence or that of something spiritual about me and I would think of that old hymn we used to sing in Sunday School.

" And he walked with me and he talked to me
And he tells me that I am his own".

Somehow that walk in the woods renewed me. It made things better, I would come back home from the woods transformed, feeling my problems were after all .. small .. and the world was a better place. It was much like waking up after a good night's sleep.

Among my fondest memories were those warm spring nights when thousands of frogs serenaded us in the evening from the bush all around us, as we sat out on the veranda steps in the cool of the evening at rest after the day's work.

Soon the whole bush would resound with the croaking and trilling of hundreds and hundreds of frogs, throbbing a chorus of happiness Every now and then an old bullfrog added a rich loud croak perfecting a country in harmony as we knew it.
Later the wild crab-apple trees would burst forth in blossoms and then the leaves would appear.
In the early summer mornings the dove cooed to us from my uncle's bush.

So remember when you feel the need to refuel, to recharge your batteries, take time for
"A Walk In The Woods."

When you come back from a walk in the woods you will find your world
will seem to be a bit brighter and your path a bit smoother.

38

The Wood Cutting Bee

The Wood Cutting Bee

Late in the fall after the leaves had fallen from the trees and the fall ploughing was done, yet long before the first fallen snow we would hitch the horses to the old farm wagon and drive to the bush to bring in our winter wood.

The old farm dog would be excited about a trip to the bush and ready to follow the wagon or to dash ahead and come back to greet us. This was one job I never minded doing, as it was not a hurried job but one done with a certain amount of leisure. If not alone one had time to chat while working. On damp days the smell of the disturbed leaves beneath your feet was ample pay for the work you were doing. Even the horses seemed to sense that there was a certain feeling of freedom in the air or was there just something pleasant about being in the bush surrounded by nature? Perhaps for us there was a good feeling within us knowing that wood was a renewable resource and for your labour you got free heat for the winter.

Most farmers cut their wood in the winter or previous spring. Mature or dying trees were cut down in the bush with a crosscut saw. Then the tops were trimmed with sharp axes, the brush piled and the limbs cut into long pieces and stood on end nearby not unlike a huge wigwam to dry all summer. The huge tree trunk itself was cut to four foot lengths then split with wedges into cord wood 4 feet long and the wood piled to dry in an open space all summer.

Stakes on the side of the wagon box allowed us to pile the wagon high with short and long pieces of wood. All the while we were working, the old farm dog checked out the many groundhog holes he knew were in the vicinity. Every now and then he came back to check on us and then off in a new direction on an adventure all of his own. Once in a while he proudly brought back a prize and dropped it at our feet, one awfully dead fat groundhog. I have never seen a dog eat one, - a rabbit yes, but a groundhog no.

Soon we would have our load on and ready to travel. All too often I found myself piling the wood too high; thus many times I had to stop to pick up something that had fallen off.

Once we arrived at the area near the house designed for the wood pile the wood would be neatly stacked or piled on end awaiting the day we would have a buzz saw bee, but for now we would return to the bush for yet another load of wood followed by a happy dog.

Every fall my dad would have a woodcutting bee. Those who helped us would sooner or later call on us to come to their place for their woodcutting bee. It was very much a social gathering of old friends and we enjoyed working together.
As a rule my dad would have a couple of neighbours. It would most often be Ed Smith and Norman Morrison, or perhaps Ernie or Bill Roger.

My dad always had a circular saw for as long as I remember, so he always wanted to be the one to stand behind the blade and make the cuts. As for me the farther away I was from the blade the better. Ya! yes, I guess I was chicken?

When everyone was appointed their job and all was ready they ran the wood through the circler saw. This wood was for both the furnace and the kitchen wood stove. To run smoothly it took 3 or 4 men. A couple of guys would bring the long pieces of wood from the woodpile where it was stacked and slide it down onto the board at the rear of the circler saw. Each time dad pushed the board forward the saw cut off a foot of wood. I would often have to hold the end of the wood steady while the cut was made and then hurry back to the stacked wood pile and tug out the next piece to be sawed.

The guy on the receiving end of the cut off foot of wood would throw it onto a pile on the ground to his left. As the day proceeded the pile of cut wood rose higher and higher in the air and the smell of fresh cut wood scented the cool fall air. There was always a lot of scary noise as the saw entered the wood. On a small piece of wood it was almost over as soon as it started as the saw made a rapid ...zing.... and it was done. On the larger pieces of hard maple, elm or beech it would enter the wood with a shrill reverberation, which soon became deafening to the ears. In a short time it would pull the saw speed down to a tormented howl and often ended in a smoking squeal. Sometimes the belt would slip and the smell of a burnt belt filtered into the cool fall air. At other times the belt would fly off the pulley and scare us. I was never comfortable working around a buzz saw. I had strange visions of a shattered saw blade being thrown into the air.

Until the 1930's and on into the 1940's farmers relied on wood for the furnace and cook stove. As times got better on the farm in the late 1940's coal was used for heat, and soon after that fuel oil. The wood cook stove gave way to an electric stove and with that we were able to enjoy a cool kitchen in the summer time. While the wood heat was economical it was not always satisfying as often the furnace fire was long out before morning. If so, then we had to use kindling to re-light it.

Still all who have cut wood in the bush, and all those who have hauled it to the wood yard to stack for a future wood bee, know a love of wood. We cannot help but remember wood heat. We are aware that there was a certain charm, a certain romance to the warmth and a smell that was so natural. There was something just right that cannot be captured by the modern heat we have today.

The Love Of

Old Barns

The Love Of Old Barns

The Cooke - Barn - Driving Shed - Hen House   by Jack

Every time I drive northward out of London I feel I am heading home. As I view the familiar countryside my mind wanders back to those yesteryears when the world seemed new and my whole life was still before me. So much in our lives has changed. I like to believe it has changed for the better, but there was a cost. Along the way we lost the old-fashioned charm and wonder that enriched our daily lives and kept us close to nature. Now we live in a tidy, sterile world of our own making, and we cannot turn back the clock.

For better or for worse we once shared our lives with nature all about us.

The country is still beautiful but somewhere deep within me is a hunger for something that is not there. Life has changed in the country and down on the farm. Perhaps it is for the best. Yet memories of another world flood my mind of times when living on the farm was not a job but simply a chosen way of life. Many people did not want to be enslaved by others or other people's hours. They only asked to work at what they loved, free of intrusion.

What I miss the most are those huge old weathered wide hemlock board barns, which at one time dominated every farm throughout rural Ontario. Built in the late 1800's or in the early 1900's they capture the imagination of everyone who loved the farm. Besides being charming and serviceable they were simply bird and animal friendly. Mind you, not all of those who took up residence in and around the barn were exactly welcome, but most birds won acceptance or were simply put up with.

Originally most of our barn birds were not North American birds to start with, but were introduced to this country by the Europeans in the mid or late 1800's. Some people simply missed the birds from home. Starlings introduced in Central Park, New York in the 1890's was one big mistake. Within 50 or 60 years they became a pest all the way to the west coast. The bird we call the English Sparrow is really a Finch and called a House Sparrow in Europe. Rock Pigeons common in Europe became our common Barn Pigeon.

I grew up in a wooded area of rural Ontario where barn birds fitted into our everyday lives around the barn as naturally as the rest of the birds fitted into that wooded area and swamp all about us. Most of us today visualize only the furry critters that called a barn home without thinking of all our feathered friends. Who could imagine a barn without horses and cows, pigs and ever so many cats? Life around the barn would not be complete without the barn birds. It all went together to create a kind of harmony, which made life around the barn complete ----- horses, cows, pigs, cats and birds.

At one time almost every farm had a variety of livestock and crops. To house that stock and the crop they had to have a large bank barn. A bank barn is one that has stables and pens below to house the horses, cattle and hogs and a second floor above for straw, hay and grain to feed and bed them.

It is called a bank barn because it has a large bank of earth built to the rear of the barn for wagons to haul load after load of hay and grain in to be used as winter-feed for the stock below. As a rule there were four big wide board doors hung on huge hinges that opened wide, The doors ran from the ground to the eave under the roof. All summer long our horses hauled load after load of hay and sheaves of grain up that bank and into the barn. Enjoying the fruits of our labour were the birds who made this barn their home.
There were always kernels of grain for food and abundance of fibre for nests.

A barn was always the centre of activity on the farm. In the early morning we did the milking and fed the stock. After the morning or evening chores were done, life went on for its freeloader tenants. The pigeons cooed, made love and preened themselves on the very peak of the barn roof. The barn sparrows sang from the rafters while others continued to build their nests under the eaves. Now that the cows and the farm hands had left the stable the barn swallow went back to work building its nest. The cats sat nearby, lazily washing each other's faces after burying their heads deep into the froth on the pails of skim milk.

The barn provided comfort and shelter for all those within for over one hundred years. It endured the scorching summer heat, the wild storms of summer of wind, rain and hail. It was a shelter from the sub-cold in winter. All those within snuggled down feeling safe from the summer storm or the winter's blast of the wind and the deepest snow. The farmer came and went. The pigeons cooed. The sparrows chirped and sang from morn till dawn. Such was life, once upon a time, in the barn.

Once The Very Heart Of Every Farm Enterprise

Old Barns Are Fast Disappearing

Billy Our Farm Goat

Billy Our Farm Goat

The first goat I can ever remember being introduced to, was the goat that belonged to my mom's brother, my Uncle Loril Butson at Munro. The village of Munro is just a few miles south of the town of Mitchell, Ontario on Highway 23. No, I don't remember the name of the goat and I am not sure he ever had one.

We had been invited to a Sunday dinner at Uncle Loril and Aunt Pearl's. A Sunday dinner at Aunt Pearl's was always a wonderful, fulfilling event.

At the dinner table the conversation turned to my Uncle Loril's new investment, a billy goat. Up until then I don't think I had ever seen a goat, at least not one up close. At about 8 or 10 years old I was very anxious to see it, as I already knew I loved all animals. Uncle Loril said we would go to the barn right after dinner.

Many years ago it seems there were a lot of farmers who thought that when they kept a goat in the barn it would ward off diseases in their stock. Some even thought it brought them good luck. I am sure there is no real proof in any of this, but many believed if a goat were put in with cattle the cows would not abort. In the same way they believed sheep would be disease free if a goat was allowed to run free with them. Perhaps it was the smell of the goat and the fact that their goats always seemed to have a short life that led them into thinking the goat filled up with bad things and died. Still this theory had been handed down to them for many generations.

If you go to the Bible it will tell you that in Ancient Babylon, a goat was sent to die in the desert in order that it would carry away the sins and diseases from the people: ***"and the Hebraic scapegoat was driven into the wilderness, taking away the sins of the Jews." (Leviticus 16: 21)***

After dinner my dad, Uncle Loril and I went to the barn to see the goat. Uncle Loril was a good farmer. He loved his stock and kept a nice warm, clean barn. His cattle were always in good shape, looking cared for and content. We found the goat far down the passageway tied in a small stall all by itself. He was thoughtfully chewing his cud while his eyes regarded us with cool intelligence. He was a handsome critter as goats go, mostly black with two great horns curved back toward his neck. The horns had large ridges unevenly spaced along their length. Each ridge represents one year of growth. He had a long handsome beard on his chin. He seemed quite content to look, but yet still ignored us. There was no wag of the tail or forward movement of his ears. It was as if he was waiting for one of us to make the first move. Uncle Loril advised me not to touch him as he might hurt me. I think all this only made me all the more interested in him. Boys like adventure. Boys like a dare.

Some time later my dad decided he too should buy a goat to protect his livestock from diseases and whatever else it was that goats were supposed to do for us or be good for. Of course I was happy about this? So far I was a friend of all our farm animals so why not add a goat to all that. I had found my Uncle Loril's goat interesting but not very hospitable. I dreamed of owning a goat. I would be a good friend. A ten-year-old boy gets tired of playing with his sisters. I needed a billy goat.

Sure enough, one day dad came home with a big black billy goat in his trailer. He was even bigger then my uncle's goat and 10 times as fierce. Dad had a short rope on him and he fought dad all the way to his stall in what we called the middle stable. He may have been considered a handsome brute by those nannies at his former residence wherever it was he came from, but he was one mean spirited billy goat the day he landed on our farm and certainly not a happy camper.

Grandma said he smelled like sin and acted like the very devil. He was extremely rank and musty and yet he was strangely compelling. Perhaps that was because he was mad and yet seemed completely fearless of the world about him. His actions were so strange toward us. We loved animals and most of them in time responded to us but Billy the goat boldly rejected us.

It was winter when we got him and the cattle were in the barn. He was tied with a cattle chain in a small single stall where we had to pass by in front of him every time we entered the barn. Each time anyone came near he would rear up and come crashing down on the headboard across the front of his stall. I thought in time he would tame down and we could befriend him. Most goats are social animals and get along well with other farm animals, cats, horses and cattle and yes,... people. Dogs can be their worst enemy, but dogs are easily trained not to harm them. It just seemed our Billy didn't want or need a friend; I think he was born with more than one burr under his tail.

We never won him. Thus to us he always remained a mystery. If you tried to befriend him in any way he would butt at you viciously and threaten you with his horns. He was never thankful for a treat, and showed no affection for anyone.

Goats are herd animals so dad had hoped in the spring he could let the goat run free with the cows. When spring came he turned him loose with the cows. While he got along fine with the cattle it was not safe for me to fetch the cows, to bring them in for milking.

The goat ended up on the end of two long heavy logging chains fastened to a huge maple tree stump in the laneway. The chain I know was much too heavy for him to carry about but by now my dad had little sympathy for him. He soon ate the orchard grass from all around the stump to the bare ground and was reaching far out for what was out of reach to him. This caused the heavy chain to cut into his neck and I am sure caused him a lot of pain. On hot days there was no shade at the stump for him and by mid-day the sun grew very hot. I know now that goats suffer in the hot sun as they sunburn easily and they need shade. Let us say we didn't understand much about goats and it seems this goat didn't try to understand us.

For the most it seemed my dad lost interest in the goat and left it up to me, a kid to care for him. Like all kids I had a very bad memory at times and besides I was afraid to go to near him. Often he was in need of water and fresh pasture. It was sad but he gathered little sympathy all because he was too mean to let anyone near him. Regardless he was not going to be subdued. Billy goats are very tough animals.

I still think of him yet as the king of the stump. He would stand up on his rear legs and do a little dance on the stump whenever I went out the lane to water him or to get the mail. He reared up several times to a great height threatening me and then came flying out from the stump to the end of his chain and crashed his horn into the ground. I tell you it was just scary and he knew he scared us.

We had him for several years and nothing much changed. He remained king of the stumps all summer and guarded his stall with sledgehammer blows from his horns all winter. Sometimes I wonder if he was just like some people who can't get along with others. Being "The Boss" they got all the satisfaction in life that was needed.

One fine day my dad was to drive my grandparents to Woodstock for the day to visit my grandma's sister.
In the early afternoon the sky to the northwest started to darken up. Soon we heard long rolling thunder amid flashes of lightning. I remember standing on the sidewalk with

mom and my sisters watching black rolling clouds approaching from the northwest. As the weather had been hot day and night nearly all the windows in the old brick house were open. With the storm approaching the first thing mom had to do was rush to every room in the house and close the windows. Mom ushered us into the safety of the house and then ran up the staircase to shut all the windows throughout the house. This gave me a good chance to get back outside to watch the action. At that time I was fascinated by a good thunderstorm just as I am today. I stood on the veranda hugging the post next to the steps. I had little fear, as I knew God was putting on this great show just for me. The rain poured down and the wind roared as it picked up debris and tree branches and hurled them through the air. What a show. I was simply thrilled from head to toe until my mother grabbed me by the shirt collar and literally tossed me into the kitchen.

I am sure by now my mom expected it was more then just the usual summer thunderstorm. She probably expected the coming of a tornado. Mom knew the old back kitchen built onto the main house was not the safest place for us to stay, so she herded us into the front hall where we all sat on the lower steps and waited.

Soon we heard a terrible banging coming from the dining room. After a second and third and fourth bang we all left our sheltered spot and ventured close behind my mom into the dining room to find out what was making the noise. When we looked out the dining room window onto the front veranda there was Billy our huge old billy goat standing on the veranda. Somehow he had got loose from his chain on the stump in the laneway.

Naturally we were all afraid of him and we didn't want him in the house. It seemed strange that now in the midst of a terrible storm he came to us for protection. He was simply terrified and wanted in, out of the storm. He banged his head on the front door as only a billy goat can do. Mom knew he would break the door down and come in, if she could not get him to go away.

There was a large pot of very hot water on the back end of the kitchen stove. Mom carried the hot water to the dining room door and opened it and threw it on poor old Billy's head. He dashed off the veranda shaking his head and we didn't see him again until after the storm. It was a sad thing to have to do; poor Billy.

Billy the goat survived and was soon enjoying the pasture along the lane once more. Many trees were downed in the lane by that tornado and we ended up with many more flat top stumps from those trees. These stumps became his domain, and he became king of many stumps. He stood on top of every stump and reared and shook his angry head and challenged anyone to dare come near him.

Billy lived for a few more years but never yielded an inch. He died in his stall a tragic death. He apparently broke his neck. We found him one morning with one horn stuck behind the upright piece of wood his chain ring was fastened to. It seemed his horn got stuck behind it and he threw himself, time and time again, to get free. By doing this he eventually broke his neck. It was a sad ending for a sad life. Sometimes it does not pay to be too ornery. We all need friends.

We never invested in another billy goat. I learned to appreciate my sisters.

The moral of the story is:
It is better to have three good sisters then one bad goat.

Grandpa's Red Durham Cows

Grandpa's Red Durham Cows

I like to think that many years ago there was something special, perhaps even magical about birth on the farm, be it new born calves, little pigs, kittens, little chickens or baby birds. As a child I witnessed them all with awe and wonder. With the exception of little kittens nothing on the farm at that time was mass-produced.
Birth on the average farm was never recorded but every birth was indeed special.

As a small boy growing up on the farm in the nineteen thirties, nothing much escaped me. Little boys are very curious, and they learn very early in life where babies come from. None of our cows had pedigrees but they all had names. There was Suzy and Toots and Old Boots and Betty, Maude and Bertha and three nice old bossies I named after my 3 sisters Laurine, Pearl and Jean. There were times though when a milk pail got kicked over that my dad forgot the name and called them something different, but my mom told me I should not repeat it.

Soon after my dad got married in 1926 he rented the farm on the Mitchell Road from his father. Along with the farm came a herd of Red Durham cattle. Durham I understand is really a dual purpose Short Horn. This means while they made a good milk cow, if you cross them with a good short horn bull you got an excellent beef calf every year. For some reason I don't remember my dad or grandfather ever referring to them as Short Horns but always as Durham. I am sure this had something to do not only with the red cows but also with my grandfather coming from England. I understand that is where the "Durham Red" cows came from.

Coming out of the 1920's into the 1930's my grandfather had a beautiful herd of mostly Red Durham cattle. I remember when I was a very shall boy in the early to mid 30's my dad arrived home one day with a large magnificent all white Short Horn bull. My grandfather was not at all pleased to have his Red Durham cows crossed with this all white Short Horn bull. At the time I didn't understand.

However he had to admit it was a beautiful and powerful looking animal. This bull often scared the living daylights out of me when he got frisky and tore about in his stall. I was sure one day he might get loose and hurt or even kill someone. He wore a specially made chain around his neck which was fastened to a large ring that slid up and down on a piece of Ironwood my grandfather had cut from an Ironwood tree in our bush. After shaving it with the drawing knife and hand carving it to fit, my grandpa bolted it upright to the heavy planked siding of the stall. The bull wore a big shiny brass ring in his nose. I always like to think he wore it with pride. For a number of years the white bull sired calves from our red cows.

My grandpa was right about the white bull cross with his cows as after a number of years it had a disastrous effect on my grandfather's herd of beautiful Red Durham cattle. Most of the new stock was no longer red. There were a few white cattle and a muddle of roan. Some were red cattle with white spots but no more solid red heifers to add to the herd. Only a few older red cows were left.

I know my grandfather was not happy about the way things turned out, but it didn't seem to bother my dad. He never seemed to care about the breeding of good stock and mocked those who did. He even added a few Holsteins and crossbred them to his Short Horn bull. After a number of years we ended up with a crappy looking herd with a bit of everything.

My best memories were of those early to mid-thirties when our herd consisted mainly of my grandfather's cattle of large bodied but gentle Red Durhams. They were tied by chain two in a double stall to a well-worn heavy plank partition. Ten cows tied in a row filled what was called the cow stable. In front was a heavy wooden plank manger with a division in the center to keep one cow from sampling the other cow's dinner. The cows were turned out once a day in the forenoon to drink water from the well behind the barn. As I got a few years older it was my job to pump the water into the wooden trough. I would pump and I would pump and those old red cows grew bigger and bigger until they looked like walking barrels. After filling themselves with very cold water they stood looking very cold and uncomfortable at the gate wanting back into the warm barn.

Behind the cows was a six-inch deep gutter in which the cows were supposed to do their business. Some cows are very clean that way and others didn't seem to care just where they went. By now you will be aware that little boys are not only curious but they are also very observant. Before the cows would be let back into the stable the gutter had to be cleaned and fresh wheat straw bedding put in the stalls. My dad inherited my grandpa's old wheel barrel and would you believe it, we used it all the years I was on the farm up until 1960 and then it was sold along with the farm to the new owner the Penners. The last time I remember seeing it was in 1961when Fred was giving his brother Dave a ride up the manure pile and dumping him.

At that time it was just natural for the farmer to allow his cows to follow the nature of all animals in the wilds, so the cows gave birth to calves in the spring.

My earliest adventure in witnessing the birth of a calf was of course quite by accident, and as I remember it a startling but memorable scene. One morning I donned my duds and headed out to the barn uninvited.
My dad was too busy to notice me arrive. He had two hame straps from the horse harness on the legs of the calf, which was half way out of the cow. The cow gave a final push and my dad gave a pull and suddenly a whole wet-looking calf slid out onto a bed of straw behind the cow.

I stood there with my eyes wide open and I expect my mouth too. My dad gave the calf a quick rub down with a burlap grain sack and put his fingers into the calf's mouth to clear it of fluid. Then an all wet red calf struggled to its feet and on wobbly legs was trying to nurse on its mother, The poor mother chained to the stall was trying as best it could to reach the calf…. to lick it clean of fluid. Had we known in those days what we know now we would have unchained the cow and let her lick the calf. We know now that this liquid is Mother Nature's very best remedy to ease the mother's birthing pains and help her to settle down.

It seems this fluid on the calf acts as a pain reliever to the cow after giving birth much as ASA acts on humans.

The licking also stimulates the calf's blood and makes the calf warm and stronger fast so that it is soon up on its legs. A lot of newborn calves could have had a better start at life if we had been better informed.

Today we also know that the calf should have the first mother's milk as soon after birth as possible. Again this new milk is Mother Nature's own protection for many things. It protects the calf from intestinal bacterial infections, which is the cause of white scours that kill many calves.

I know as a little boy I asked my dad a lot of questions that morning. I thought I had a right to know and that it was necessary to know. After all we lived on a farm. I realize now that my dad was uncomfortable at my presence and thought I should not be there. He was not good at answering my questions at the best of times and certainly no good at a time like this. Then again it was a fact; my dad was just not a morning person. Every morning he woke up angry at the world and never wanting to talk before he had his breakfast. How I wish we had a Tim Hortons close by for him in those days.

In the 1930's health care of livestock was not a big issue. It was sort of potluck. You won some and you lost some. All too often home remedies were applied which did more harm then good. When the calf or cow was almost dead the final decision was made to call the vet. Of course then when the cow died you knew whom to blame.

All farmers had to watch their calves carefully for calf scours. This is a bacterial infection in the intestines. It can quickly destroy cells and enter the blood stream and be fatal for the calf. It seemed that every farmer had his very own remedy to help the calf, but most were quite simple. First they had to find just the right bottle, a bottle with a long neck. Remember now, pop bottles like we have today had not been invented yet and it seemed that most things that came in bottles came with a stubby neck. Bottles like that they called a medicine bottle. Dad would fill the bottle half full of skim milk and then put in three whole eggs to which he added a swig of cod liver oil. Shake this until its well mixed, then give it to the calf. This is what they called drenching.

You would soon find out that the calf had no idea of making this easy for you. Calves will readily suck on your fingers, but they can be very stubborn. So what you have to do is back the calf into a corner of the pen, then put your hand over its nose and hold its head upright with your two fingers in its mouth to suck on. You insert the mouth of the bottle to the side of the mouth all the while holding the calf to the side of the pen with your body. You slowly try to fool the calf into sucking on your fingers while tilting the bottle with your home made remedy up to allow the gooey substance to go down into its throat. Of course it does not taste too good and the calf will fight you but patience usually wins in the end.

It seems cows soon forget their calves, if they never get a chance to bond. Our cows were kept mainly for milking and a good calf was considered a bonus every year. This means the calf has to learn to drink milk from a pail. When you try to teach a calf to drink milk from a pail you become very aware God put its head on wrong. Nature makes the calf want to drink milk as a calf drinks from the cow with its head up. A calf suddenly has the strength of a full-grown bull when you try to force its head down into a pail. To start a calf to drink from a pail you first back it into a corner in its pen. Then with your body you crowd it against the wall so you're in control.
In one hand you carry a pail with a small amount of milk. Place your hand on the calf's face as before when drenching. Slide your hand down over the nose and into the mouth. The calf will immediately start to suck on your fingers. Now with all your might bend the head down. You will never know how strong a little calf is until you try to force that head down.

It is important to allow it to breathe, as you don't want to get milk into its lungs. So force the head down and then let it up, then down again and let it up. Be firm but don't expect great things the first couple of times. It is important that it gets something in its tummy, but hunger will work in your favour so be patient.

Calves and children go together like pie and ice cream, it just seems they were meant for each other. I believe every child is a better person if they learn to love… …and earn the love of animals. I am sure it is what the good Lord expected of us.

My Grandpa's Orchard

My Grandfather's Orchard

When you speak of apples to most people now-a-days they have immediate visions of bright red, green and yellow apples all neatly stacked in show cases in the local super-market. Little do they know of the history of the apple tree or realize the historic importance of the apple to our forefathers the pioneers.

Can you imagine our forefathers putting in several months of winter in their log house often ten and twenty or more miles from the nearest town? Some may have been lucky enough to have a local general store within a few miles but when it came to fruit in winter the pickings were very thin.

Our history books give little credit to those special few who brought with them livestock such as cattle, horses, pigs and chickens, and even less to those who brought with them seeds of every kind from corn to oats and barley to winter wheat. Then again there were those special few who in great foresight brought such things as apple trees and apple seed.

We have all heard it said, "As Canadian or As American As Apple Pie" and it is true, they were raised on apple pie, apple puddings and apple sauce.

My grandfather arrived in Canada from Peterborough England in 1886 via New York City. He made his way north to London so he would be close to his brother Will and sister Emma who were already living here in London.

For a few years my grandfather rented a farm near Woodstock. It was there he got his start at farming in Canada. In 1893 he married Alice Collins formally of Maidstone of Essex County near Windsor.

My grandmother's forefathers the Collins family emigrated from England in 1807 first to New York City and then to Michigan. Being English the war of 1812 put them in an awkward position so they joined the throng of Empire Loyalists and moved to Maidstone in Essex County of Southern Ontario.

My grandmother was visiting her sister, my Aunt Maimie, who lived in Woodstock and that was where my grandfather met her.

My Grandfather George E Cooke married my Grandmother Alice P Collins in 1892 in Woodstock.

Somewhere in that area he rented a farm and the first three of their four children were born there. Bertha was born in 1894 and George in 1895. John my dad was born in 1898.

In 1899 my grandfather drove north from Woodstock with his horse and buggy in search of a farm to buy. He found a farm he liked west and north of the village of Motherwell on the new Mitchell Road. Lot 22 and part 23 W.

It had a brand new huge white brick story and a half house with five bedrooms, just what my grandfather needed for his family.

However I sometimes like to think that perhaps it was also because of the well-established apple orchard that he bought this farm.

For many years most of the trees in the orchard were very productive and my grandfather shipped many wooden barrels of apples to England. Unfortunately he, like many other farmers did not understand how to manage an apple orchard. As the years went by many of the trees were non-productive. While my grandfather enjoyed his orchard in his own way he left it more or less to survive on its own. He was a good gardener and he kept a large vegetable garden with a patch of asparagus and a lot of great rhubarb.

When I was a child in the 1930's my grandfather's orchard was very much a matured, overgrown orchard. I say overgrown because the trees had never been pruned or cut back. They were huge and by now getting very old. However to me as a child these trees really looked, as apple trees should. They were trees with large trunks and low spreading limbs, - limbs which invited you as a child to climb about and play until you eventually fell out onto the ground, just as your mother had warned you.
These strong limbs were also just right for swings of all sizes. As a small child I spent many hours sitting on a swing in the shade of the old apple tree. I loved that old orchard and I knew each tree by heart, I can still picture each and every tree to this day.

Every spring I would anxiously await for the blossoms to appear for as a child I looked upon this with wonder and delight. There in our orchard for a number of days each spring were ever-blooming clouds of blossoms from one end of the orchard to the other. Robins sang cheerfully as they made their nest or fed their young amid the great bundles of blossoms. Fragrant scents drifted down to us under the trees. We walked under the cloud of blossoms with their many shades from white to pink, which in the distance drifted off into a soft purple hue. The drone of honey bees and happy song of birds filled the air and made all this seem, ... a promise for a fruitful year.

Each year I watched and I waited for the gift they would bear. I like to think this orchard gave up its apples willingly with pride and joy as I felt these trees knew my grandfather and me as well as we knew the trees.

For reasons unknown to us at that time some of the trees never bore much fruit. However there were always all the apples we needed for ourselves, - spies for pies, harvest apples for applesauce and mom's great apple pudding. There were snows for early eating in the fall and Thomas Sweets and Russets, which kept well all winter. In the mid summer there was a wonderful eating apple right outside my grandparent's kitchen window called Yellow Transparent. In the late summer a red apple called the St Lawrence always arrived about grain threshing time. Almost every farm in our area started out with an very good orchard, but over the years they too like my grandfather's trees grew old and slowly died off.

Apples it seems have existed as wild fruit since prehistoric times and were cultivated for more then 3000 years by the Greeks the Romans and the Egyptians. It is believed they learned much about their apples trees and how to graft trees from China. Sad though is the fact that when the Greek and Roman Empires were over run by barbarians and they entered into what is often referred to as the dark ages, literacy and craftsmanship were lost. Thus many years later when the first settlers from Europe came to America the average farmer knew little or nothing about the care of apple trees, or how to successfully graft a tree. They had to start from scratch with the little knowledge they had.

The French in Nova Scotia made great headway growing apples. They soon understood that apple trees were cross-pollinators, meaning they require the pollen from another tree preferably of a different kind in order to produce fruit. They had also found out that when you plant the seed from an apple you never get the mother tree but rather some other tree because of the cross- pollination. Nevertheless this by chance system produced many of to-days apples, which includes the granddaddy of all apples found at Dundela Ontario near Ottawa the McIntosh apple.

Trees from Nova Scotia spread along the St Lawrence River into what is now Quebec and south into the United States. Credit is given to The United Empire Loyalist for introducing many of the apple trees to Southern Ontario. By the late 1880's to 1900 it is said there were over 80 varieties of apples growing in Ontario.

In the mid nineteen thirties, possibly in the extreme hot summer of 1936 a tornado destroyed much of grandfather's orchard. Fortunately a few of the best trees survived. When my dad sold the farm in 1961 there were about six trees left. Today the old orchard is no more and it is the same across much of the country today. While an apple tree can live for over 100 years most trees today are only kept in production for 20 to 30 years and then replaced.

Across the country in Ontario there are pleasant reminders of what used to be. There are many woodlots with areas of neglected orchards or perhaps a pasture field with an old wild apple or crab-apple tree. These trees continue to produce fruit for wild life, such as the birds, the racoons, rabbits and the deer.

There are few old apple trees left on farms today, to wander beneath and remember my grandpa and his orchard, and the yesteryears.

> Some keep the Sabbath going to church, I keep it staying at home.
> With a bobolink for a chorister, and an orchard, for a dome.
> Emily Dickinson, 1862

Profound Deafness

Profound Deafness

The Doctor told me, in time I would suffer "Profound Deafness." This sudden bareness of the ultimate truth meant that there was no hope for a cure. It was unacceptable for an active young man in his early teens.

Winter had arrived early in the fall of 1942 and by December we were deep in snow. Already our school and church were practising skits, songs and plays for our annual Christmas concerts. Early snows in the 1940's were very seasonable. By December our world was white and this served its purpose to introduce the coming of yet another Christmas season.

Unknown to us our practice for this year's Christmas concerts were in vain.

Scarlet Fever somehow came to our house that early winter of 1942. Although it is supposed to be very contagious we were the only family in the community to get it. Where it came from we will never know. Within a few days my three sisters and I all came down with it. It is an infection caused be streptococcus bacterium transmitted through the air or personal contact. Scarlet Fever usually infects young children. This strain of bacteria can cause a toxic shock syndrome, which is why the skin turns red. Every inch of your body is covered with this sandpaper like red rash even on your lips and the inside your mouth nose and ears. The throat is very sore.

Perhaps one day after the disease had been confirmed a man walking up onto the veranda to the kitchen door, without saying hello pounded nails into a heavy cardboard sign, which said, "Under Quarantine – No Admittance."
For several weeks this separated us from the outside world. During the early 1900's there were many serious outbreaks of scarlet fever. It is a very rare disease today. The theory being that this strain of bacteria has become weaker over time.

I remember that my grandfather had died in the spring of 1941 and my grandmother had gone to Detroit to live with her youngest daughter, my Aunt Maude. This left one part of the main floor of the farmhouse vacant. My mom set up beds in what used to be my grandparent's bed room and kitchen so she could look after all four of us and not have to climb the tall staircase to the second floor of the old farm house all day. I was put on a cot in what used to be my grandparent's kitchen. I found that part very comforting. My three sisters were in what used to be my grandparent's bedroom.

The doctor had told my mom to put us to bed, to keep us covered and very still. I would be 14 years old and my sisters Jean and Pearl younger and Laurine one year older. Can you imagine trying to keep four kids at that age in bed and still? I don't mean for a day but for days on end. In those days everyone thought you had to break a fever by sweating it out. Thus when you had a fever they piled more and more quilts on you. I remember being so very hot and wet with sweat so I kept taking my quilts off and my mom kept putting them back on. There was no Medicare at that time and little money to spend on medical needs, so for the most parents stuck to old fashion remedies. That might mean a mustard plaster or Rawleigh's liniment. That's just how it was

All four of us were very ill and there was little or no money for medicine. I remember dad went to see Dr. Pridham in despair and upon getting home he went straight out into the orchard with his shovel and dug up curled dock roots. The weed was easy to find as it stood out against the snow covered ground growing in clumps of brown winter drab stalks here and there across the orchard. Most Country doctors were well aware that the Indians used many plants for their medical needs. Among them was the water from the boiled curled dock roots for sore throat and itching skin. Mom washed the tuber like roots and boiled them in water. When she thought it was done we drank the murky brown water as medicine to cure our sore throats and to stop the itching. I can't tell you how good it was as a medicine but for the moment it sure took our thoughts away from our ailment. Still I feel it was good for us.

My sister Pearl and I both lost our hearing because of the damage caused by this fever. I often wonder if fewer quilts would have saved us from the damage done by the fever. However that was as the doctor recommended in those days.

Pearl's and my hearing loss came on quite rapidly. Soon I started to fall behind in my schoolwork. As we neared the end of the school year my teacher Miss Ida McMillan started to keep me in after four to catch up on the day's work. As she put it, she was not going to let me fail. She made me work hard so that I would pass my final grade eight exams. I am not sure that I knew how to appreciate it at that age, but years later I came to realize what she did for me. With over fifty students in eight grades, in a one-room school it was hard for a teacher to find time to give individual attention to a student. Yet I know she did this for me. I am aware now she cared about the students she taught. She was not just teaching to the rules.

I was having earaches and noise problems while at school and in the evening I found comfort in wrapping a hot flat iron in a towel and holding it to my ear. Flat irons were always available at that time as they were left on the rear of the kitchen stove all the time. I would go to bed with one on my ear and the other at my feet on a cold winter night. Thus for a little while I was warm at both ends.

I did pass my exams and got into high school, but it was not long before I realized that I could not keep up as all the teaching was done verbally. I did not too bad until after Christmas, when I started to notice that I just could not follow the teachers at all. I started to borrow other kid's homework, so much so that I noticed they started to avoid me. It got to the place they just could not keep doing it as it was affecting their own studies.

All the time my hearing was getting worse with earaches and noise. One day while sitting at my desk in school my ears suddenly went pop -- a kind of sudden explosion, which left me with a big hollow ringing within my head much like when you shoot off a shot gun. My room teacher Peter Pigeon was a cousin by marriage and he was aware I was having a problem. I explained to him that something had happened ... my ears had popped and now I had a funny feeling. He sent me down the street to a family doctor, Dr. Pridham. The doctor looked in my ears and told me that one eardrum was totally gone and the other was shattered. Knowing that I had scarlet fever he told me that my nerve endings were severely damaged and were dying off. Within a few years and I would be left with "Profound Deafness".

That was I think the first time that it really sank in. I was going deaf. I was going to spend most of my life without hearing.

He doubted very much that my drums would ever heal. This was a problem to me as it let hurting and indistinguishable noise into the inner ear and at first I would jump at the first word anyone said and soon I became a nervous wreck. It is hard to explain how I was losing my hearing and yet I was being shocked by noise. This was because the noise entered my shattered eardrum onto damaged nerve endings. The noise was just that, 'noise' not sounds that were normal. It was just before Easter that this happened, and I believe the year was 1944. That was the end of my education. M.P. sons and other notaries were made aware that the government would pay for the education of their deaf children at that time, but no one came forward to tell me a farmer's son about it. I think now that surely someone could have came forward and guided me to the school for the deaf. I have often wondered just what I might have done in life if I had got an education, or if I at least I had my hearing. However it was not to be.

I know I was very depressed for a number of years and lost for direction but that was about to change for in a letter to her aunt in Alberta my mom explained my problem. My aunt asked if they would let me go out and see if the dry air would help me. Actually my Aunt Rosena believed in Christian Science and wanted to help me. I was 15 coming 16 the fall of 1944 when I took the train out west to Alberta. That trip opened up an all-new life for me.

I fell in love with the west and all the people that I came in contact with. The people I worked with seemed to overlook my hearing loss and I found the more at ease I was the better my hearing seemed to be. Actually it was some time before I realized that I was beginning to lip-read people more and more as my hearing got worse.

Now it is many years later and at times I question life.

I wonder how many people don't look back upon life and wonder…
What if… <u>this</u> had not happened?
Or what if <u>that</u> had not happened? I am sure we all do.

    Recently I wrote a book entitled, "Getting By In A Silent World."
    Writing that book was … as I put it the labour of love. Perhaps by penning your own life story you are better able to stand back and view a whole lifetime, and ask, "What If?"

    Many people have come to me and said, "In spite of your deafness what a wonderful life you have had." It has made me realize that it was so.

    I have spent much of the year working on the family tree; it will be finished for Christmas. I found out many things about the Cooke family. One thing I found very interesting was the family motto

"Tu ne cede malis, sed contra audentior ito"
Yield not to misfortunes, but go more boldly against them

Taking

Uncle Guy

Fishing

Taking Uncle Guy Fishing

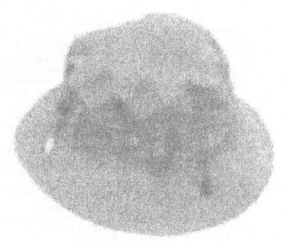

Many years ago in the mid 1930's my dad's youngest sister, my Aunt Maude met her second husband Guy Starks, while working in the Ford Hospital in Detroit. Eventually she decided it was time to bring him up to meet the family in Canada.

My 3 sisters and I were very excited, as we all loved our Aunt Maude dearly. On the morning of the day they were to arrive all four of us sat by the upstairs' bedroom window, looking far to the south down the Mitchell Road all the way to the United Church towering in the distance. We impatiently watched and waited for their arrival. Every now and then we would see a cloud of dust on the gravel road far in the distance. We could see the dust long before we could actually see the car. As that cloud of dust grew near our spirits soared, only to be dashed again.

Finally out of the dust we recognized the car we were looking for. I can see them arriving now in their shiny 1935 two door green Ford sedan.

In those days people didn't just sit and wait for you to knock on the door. On the farm we didn't have a lot of company so when someone came to visit we were overjoyed to see them, and showed it. We kids, that is my 3 sisters and I, all bounded down the steps from the veranda onto the walk and out into the yard followed by mom and dad. Already the chief farm crier our old farm dog Toby was barking and running circles around the car. It was his job to let us know when we had company and he never let us down. Everyone got a very loud greeting.

No doubt about it. It was a royal welcome. The kind they would long remember.

When Uncle Guy got out of the car we didn't know quite what to make of him as he was a real city slicker, perhaps the first one I had ever met. He was cleaner than any farmer I had ever known. He carried a great looking walking stick and his shoes were shiny. His shirt and pants were pressed without a wrinkle to be seen. I was sure my Aunt Maude must have found him in the show window of some large down town store. On top of his head was a strange round woven straw hat such as I had never seen before. Years later I would see Bing Crosby and a few show people wearing them. He was really dressy, especially for out here on the farm, and for certainly that night the cows were in for a surprise.

Although he was the most citified uncle I had he may have been one of the easiest to get to know and to chat with. Very soon we all learned to love our Uncle Guy.

Uncle Guy liked to fish and while the Americans knew little about Canada in the 1930's they did know that it was where the fish were.

Uncle Guy had a southern accent that I liked very much. He talked with a southern drawl and he often answered you by saying, "No kidding". The very second day of his visit he asked if I could show him where the fish were.

Now if he had asked where the river was I might have understood him better. I didn't know anything about fish and fishing Fish as I knew were all in the river, just as the cows were in the pasture. I thought he would know that. It never occurred to me that as a stranger he didn't know where the Thames River was.

Now you must understand I didn't come from a fishing family and I was then and I am to this day, not a fisherman. My dad never fished nor my grandfather, and my mother wouldn't even cook fish from the river. It wasn't that I had never fished it was just that I had no interest in it. At one time my grandfather had cut me a long straight ash pole from the bush and together we skinned the bark off it. To this Grandpa attached a line, hook, cork and sinker, and I was sure it was the most beautiful of all fishing poles in the country

A few boys I knew had bamboo poles and I thought that was as good as it got.

From the trunk of his car my uncle got his shiny fishing gear with a spinning reel and all kinds of hooks and lures such as I had never seen. I can't begin to tell you as even to this day I am not a fisherman and it's all foreign to me. I won't eat most fish and especially fish caught in the local rivers.

The Thames River was a mile and a quarter due east of my dad's farm. My dad's brother my Uncle George's farm rear-ended onto the Mitchell Road right across from the front of ours. I suggested we walk to the river through my uncle's farm.

This was in the mid to late thirties and the summers of the thirties were very hot with little rain so it was very, very dry. First we had to walk through my uncle's bush swatting a thousand mosquitoes and then up a long hot dusty lane to the front of the farm. Once out of the bush the mile long lane offers no shelter from the sun

Because I was just a kid of about of about 8 or 9 at the time I'm sure my uncle thought I was lost. He kept asking, "How much farther, how much farther to the river?" Well the Thames River was just beyond the River Road, which ran in front of my uncle's barn and house. There was no short cut so in the heat and dust we plodded on. Eventually we arrived at the river and I was in for a bit of a shock by the scene before me. You see I had not been to the river all summer for as yet my mother would not allow me to go to the river to swim for fear I might drown. Now that we were here I could see that there was a really big problem. You see the river was dry. There was no water in the river bed. It was just a bone-dry hot sheet of flag stone except for the odd hole which was full of hungry mud turtles.

Mom could have safely let me go to the river alone. The worst that could have happened was for me to get eaten by hungry turtles. We walked on the river bed for a half mile south towards the village of Motherwell and then turned around and walked north for a mile towards Fullarton. Then in disgust my Uncle Guy said to me, "We might as well go home."

That was the last time he asked me to show him where the fish were.

When we arrived home my dad was waiting for us with a big smile on his face.

He asked Uncle Guy, "Where are the fish?"

To which my Uncle said, "Fish, …..we couldn't even find the water."

The

Barn Swallow

86

The Barn Swallow

Childhood Memories of the Barn Swallow bring back to me a picture of a fleeting bird forever on the go in and out of the top stable door. It was hard to get a good look at the bird, as during the day they seemed to spend far more time on the wing then sitting still. Even while building the nest they were at the nest site just a few seconds and then gone again. Swallows have it all. They are a rich satin in colour, fleet in the body and dressed with a handsome forked tail. They have a trusting nature, a friendly twitter and energy beyond the bonds of imagination.

I have never heard of anyone who did not like the swallow.

No bird that enters the barn is more trusting to humans than the Barn Swallow. Since they were here before the white man arrived and before barns were built it appears they adapted to both the barn and humans. It is known that they once made their homes high on the buffs or under cliff edges along the shores of lakes where water and insects were available. These particular little swallows were later named after the barn they adapted as their home. Barns served them well for 200 years. There are several other well known swallows such as the Cliff and Tree Swallows.

I remember in the springtime the swallow would always arrive later then any of the other birds. Few of us were aware that they had travelled far and by the time they arrived they were often completely exhausted from their long flight north. The swallow winters in Central and Southern America. When they fly north they often get caught in cold spells and late winter snow. When this happens they have to find a resting place and huddle together using their body heat to survive. Swallows do not like the cold weather. Some years many of the birds die on the long Journey north to the nest site.

Those old bank barns with the stable doors below were the ideal nesting site for the barn swallow. I suppose to them it was in a way much like entering a cave or a large hole in a cliff. These barns had large doors in two parts. All summer long the top door was left open to ventilate the barn. The great old elm log beams holding up the barn floor above was just inside the door. This was the place to attach their mud nest.

The barnyard in front of the barn offered a smorgasbord variety of flies and bugs of every description. There was only one thing they had to watch out for. That was the many barn cats that made their home here also. They were always close by, just biding their time, watching for anything with feathers and wings. Thus great care was taken to where the nest was built. It must be far out of reach of the cats.

When choosing a nest site, first they chose a wide door, one that was always left open, a place where they could enter and leave with ease. Then they preferred a large beam within a short distance from that open door. They built the mud nest on the face of the beam. To build the nest they had to have a ready supply of the right kind of mud available and of course water and other grass material for the nest. For water at our place they could visit the long wooden water trough by the pump at the rear of the barn. The right kind of mud was close at hand. It was in a small shallow ditch dug in the northeast corner of the barnyard. The ditch was intended to act as a drain for the barnyard but it never worked very well as the cattle kept trampling it in thus it was not kept clear so it would actually run.

On the east side of this little ditch just outside of the barnyard fence there was a vein of white clay with blue streaks in it. My grandfather made me aware of this place as this special clay was in a way a treasure cove. This was where he went to get a pail of clay to glaze up the inside of the wooden boards he used to plank up the holes or doors in the front of our ensilage silo.

Of course each year the swallows came back to this clay, as they knew it was perfect for building their nest. Sometimes if the old nest was in good enough shape and not too messy they would clean it out and repair the old one. Otherwise they set about building a brand new nest. They worked together tirelessly from morning till night. It seemed just as one bird arrived the other one was ready to go. It was cheerful to watch them work in so much harmony. It seemed they never fought or disagreed. They were happy to be where they were, doing what they were doing.

While the main ingredients in the nest were mud pellets they enforced it with grass, straw and in our case horsehair. In the end the nest was lined with feathers.

Once the nest is finished the female lays from 3 to 8 eggs with reddish brown spots. The incubation time for the eggs is about 14 to 16 days.
Until the baby birds hatch father stays near the nest and he sits in the nest while the mother bird leaves to feed.

Milking cows by hand can be a boring tiresome chore, so watching the swallows flying in the door to the nest and back out again seemed to help us pass the time. We reveled at the beauty of their graceful flight and their endless energy.

Joyful is the day the birds start to hatch, it is then the real work begins.

All the while they are busy feeding the brood, life goes on in the barn below the nest on the beam. The cows are milked morning and night and the other chores are done. Cows have calves and cats have kittens and people come and go. The birds though continue to go about their work, just as the farmer goes about his. There is a sort of mutual respect for each other's right, to be there, and not to be disturbed.

Life around the nest gathers speed with each new day. It is noticeably busy for the next few weeks. Even when we humans venture near the nest we are greeted with a half dozen open gapping V shaped mouths always begging for food. It seems no matter how much food their dad and mom would bring to them they were always hungry, ungrateful little creatures. In about 3weeks the brood has feathered out and are ready to take flight. Once out the door it seems they have flown the coop.

The morning came when we would arrive at the barn to do chores and all was quiet. The nest was empty and the birds were gone. For a time their constant chirping and their flight and flutter back and forth to do their thing lulled us and we all but ignored them. Now they were gone, and we missed them.

My grandfather used to plough the field with a single hand plough pulled by his favorite team of horses. The family of swallows followed them up and down the field watching for a nice juicy dinner of worms and grubs. At times they would entertain themselves by doing those wonderful rolling swooping summersaults high in the air above, all the while keeping an eagle eye on the freshly turned furrow below. Suddenly one would leave the rest and swoop down low across the furrow and snatch his dinner. At other times they would line the lane fence at the end of the field awaiting his arrival and cheerfully greet him as he ended his furrow. For a man who loved to farm, does life get better then this?

When some people drove by the field, all they would see was a lonely figure of a farmer at a boring job following his horses up and down the field. They wouldn't be aware of the friendly flutter of wings high above him or at times just over his head keeping him company. I know my grandpa was happy as he held the reins of his favorite team of horses. I can picture him now with his callused hands upon the plough handles guiding the plough up and down the field and all the while the sun shines overhead and a happy brood of young swallows follows him up and down the field.

Often when I went to get the cows a swallow would fly down on top of one of those old cedar fence posts that all farmers used to hold up the woven wire fence in their laneways many years ago. The swallow would twitter and sing to me as I walked towards it. As I neared the post it would fly to the next post just beyond … and then the next. They would do this all the way back the lane keeping me company. It seemed as if it was trying to entertain me. Or was it playing a game with me? I never quite figured it out

Perhaps the swallow looked at me as the son of their kindly landlord, and thought it had to sing for its free meals and board. Whatever I always enjoyed the show.

Every now and then we would see them all together on the local power lines or phone lines chatting up a storm. They are very much a social kind of bird and enjoy each other's company.

You would think that after so much work to raise a family they would take the rest of the year off, but no, it seems, "Nature calls." So they usually host two broods each year.

At this rate one would think that there should be a lot of swallows around, but the truth is they appear to be on a decline. With the old barns fast disappearing they have had to adjust to a new lifestyle. It seems many are managing to find new homes under bridges and freeway overpasses. Somehow I feel this is not romantic and that there is something very wrong with this picture. Never mind, some day down the road someone will be writing a story about those Bridge or Overpass Swallows and who but you will have ever heard of the Barn Swallow.

<blockquote>
Be it ever so humble, nothing can compare
To the romance of being born in a barn.
</blockquote>

<blockquote>
The swallow is not a bird that became a pest in any way.
It seemed they enjoyed being around people.
All they asked for, was a roof over their heads
A place they could safely raise their young.
In return they would enrich your life.
</blockquote>

Pete our Feathered Friend

Pete Our Feathered Friend

Pete

One morning when I was about 10 or 12, I found a young pigeon that had left its nest only to find out it could not fly. He was lucky I found him first before one of our many cats did, as he would have ended up as brunch.

I picked him up and carried him to the house where he was put in a cardboard box. He got a lot of attention from my 3 sisters and me for a few days. However my mom was not pleased to have, (as she put it) a dirty bird in the house. So it was dad that came to the rescue.

Dad had a box, which at one time was used to house a pet rabbit. It was about three feet long and two feet wide with a screen and a small door on its front. Dad hung it on the north side of what we called the gas shed. The gas shed was a small rather smelly place full of barrels of fuel for the tractor.

I didn't know how to care for a pigeon so for a while I think I over-fed it with a bit too much of everything. I remember even feeding it grass. If I remember right my mom's winter wheat became his favorite food.

We called him Pete and for once my sisters agreed with me and the name seemed to stick. At times I would put my hand in the box and try to pet him, but Pete didn't want to be petted for as yet he was too afraid of me. After a while I could see that Pete was actually warming to me and he looked forward to a visit. As Pete got a bit older and feathered out there came a day when dad said we should let him go free. Of course I didn't really want to do that as I thought of him as my pet, and if I turned him free I would surely lose him. However in my heart though I knew it was the right thing to do.

One beautiful morning we gathered in the yard to watch while I set him free. I still remember his first flight. It seemed he was aware that his time to take flight had finally arrived and he was anxious to try. On shaky wings he flew up onto the henhouse roof. The henhouse was a long lean-to that was built onto the driving shed. From there he flew up onto the driving shed roof and more or less spent the day taking in the view.

I was worried as to what would happen to him now, but there was not much we could do for Pete, as now he was on his own. Imagine our surprise for when it grew dark he flew back to his box. For his safety we locked him in every night and let him out in the morning. For some reason Pete took to dad instead of us children. I think it was because as kids we always grasped and wanted to hold onto him, where dad let him sit on his open hand. That way he didn't feel in captivity. He was still free. Whenever dad was between the house and the barn Pete would see him and fly to the henhouse roof and coo up a storm and all the while turning in rapid circles making out he was ever so mad. Dad would talk to him and he would eventually fly down onto his shoulder or head.

Many times out of nowhere he surprised dad with a visit. There would be a sudden flutter of wings and Pete was on his shoulder. Dad would put his finger up to him and Pete would make out he was fighting his finger. It really looked quite vicious. This went on for several years and I was very jealous of dad as I felt he had stolen my bird.

One spring we noted that Pete would disappear for a day or two at a time. Then one morning he came home with a beautiful lady bird. It had an all gray body but white wings. They made a charming couple. She was beautiful and we were as proud of Peter as any parent could be. We had to give Pete credit for knowing how to pick his ladies. They spent all day, everyday together in one place or another, but there was a problem. She would not spend the night with him in the box and he didn't seem to want to spend the night in the open. This was not a good arrangement. We didn't know what would eventually happen as he might lose her. However leave it to all lovebirds to find an answer.

Many years ago when my dad was a boy he had built a pigeon box high up inside the driving shed against the southeast corner. It had a hole into it from the front and also a landing board. The two lovebirds moved in there and lived happily for many years. He continued to scold my dad from high and fly down onto his head for a much-loved visit. They would do a finger and bill fight all the way to the front lawn of the house and then Pete would take off back to the driving shed.

We enjoyed Pete for many years and none of us will ever forget him, but early one winter they both disappeared at the same time. I have no idea what happened. Another winter was coming on, and they were getting old so….

I like to think maybe; just maybe, in their old age they decided to fly south.

Where Did All The Aprons Go

Where Did All The Aprons Go

A long time ago I saw a picture of a mother answering a farmhouse door to a salesman. While her hair was deshevelled and her dress well worn and faded she wore a crisp and colourful gingham apron over it. Under the apron, with just his head projecting from the one side was a small boy with an impish grin on his face. This was a typical scene on the farm all across Canada in those early years of 1930's and 40's. In those days it was hard to find a farm woman at home without an apron on. The apron was put on first thing in the morning and never taken off all day. It was often said of grandma, "No one would ever know her without her apron on."

Cotton and gingham were the preferred material for aprons if they could afford it. Some aprons went just to the waist with a large sash at the waist and ties to make a bow at the back. I remember the ones my mom made and wore the best with a bib at the top and a strap that went over the head. Young girls often wore what was called a "pinafore". It had a bib on the front and material that went round to meet at the back.

All children grew up knowing that their mother's aprons had many uses besides hiding a dingy dress. When you were very small and shy and at times the world seemed too big a place for you it was a place to hide behind from strangers. When things went wrong and you were in tears it was used to dry your eyes and at times of need, to wipe your nose. The corner end could even be moistened with spit to wipe the dirt from children's faces or hastily clean a dirty ear.

No doubt in early times the principal use of an apron may have been to hide the poverty down on the farm. In those early times not every woman could afford a nice dress to wear for everyday. A pretty, frilly apron could do wonders to hide a worn, tattered or faded dress, and besides it was functional in so many ways.

In the 1930's to the 1940's farm women started to raise little chickens for what they called their egg money. This money was spent largely on household groceries and children's spending money. Some I know ended up on the church collection plates. For their wee chicks they bought first "Chicken Starter Mash" and later "Chicken Pellets" as feed for their growing chickens. This feed came in cotton muslin sacks and the farm women took a fancy to the material in these bags, perhaps mainly because it was for free and should not be wasted.

In 1939 when World War Two came along there was a shortage of raw cotton to make the material for the soldiers' clothing and soon it was hard to find any cotton material in the local stores.

With the shortage of cotton material more and more women joined the crowd and turned to these feed sacks to help make do. They bleached and bleached until the coloured advertisement was out and the cotton turned a reasonable white. They made aprons and bed sheets and then pillowcases and tablecloths to which they added embroidered needlework. Many mothers worked late in the evening with a hoop and a needle in hand while listening to the radio with the family. That is the picture I have of my mom. They did this craft with skill and pride and worked wonders. When company came they proudly showed off their handwork.

I personally remember the bed sheets and pillowcases on my bed. Perhaps they were a little bit rough by today's standards but we were tough and we didn't complain.

There were aprons for every use whether it was donned to milk the cows or to shoo the chickens into the coop or shelters at night. In my mind's eye I can still see my grandmother and my mom out in the orchard picking up apples that had fallen from the trees and putting them into the folds of their aprons. They gathered eggs from the hen house and vegetables from the garden and even carried in wood and wood chips from the woodpile to cook dinner.

An apron could hold the hot poker to stoke the fire and then later carry the hot loaves of bread from the oven to the tabletop to cool. Hot kitchens were a norm in the summer time as they cooked everything on the wood stove. Many times the end of the apron was used to wipe sweat from the face or a sweaty brow.

Do you remember the number of flies that gathered on the screen door of the old farmhouse kitchen? When someone opened the door to come in a dozen and more flies came in along with them. Nothing, absolutely nothing, worked better to shoo the flies off the door than mother waving an apron.

Best of all when Sundays came you could always tell when special company was coming, as mom would have on her very best apron while setting the table. It was not unusual for a neighbour lady to want to help my mom with dinner, so she was handed an apron, just like that. It was a common everyday courtesy. This was not just any apron, mind you, but one made especially for a time like this, for a special guest to wear. My mom and other women I knew took great pride in making their own aprons and offering their friend a special one to wear while they were helping in the kitchen and were our guests.

Perhaps one of the more cherished memories for all men folk would be when you would be working in the backfield without a watch and your tummy was telling you that it was nearing dinnertime. You could not just quit work and wander from the field to the kitchen expecting to be fed until it was dinnertime. So you watched and waited for that old familiar sight of your mom standing in the yard or on the bank behind the barn waving her apron. This let you know dinner was ready. Whatever you were doing, mowing hay or stooking grain nothing else mattered. You stopped the tractor. You dropped the fork. Your tummy gave a sigh and your heart gave a flutter for dear old mother. After all it was now officially dinnertime, by the call of the apron.

As times got better down on the farm, there was no need to hide that dress behind an apron. It seems that aprons went out of style or favour and are all but forgotten. Many children of today have never seen their mom in an apron. In fact some may not even know just what a nice old-fashioned apron looks like.

Today, down on the farm there is no need for an apron to do the many things mom used to do. There is no wood or wood chips to pick up from the woodpile. In fact in most cases there is not even a woodpile. The apple orchards have long disappeared along with the vegetable garden. There are no little chickens to shoo into the coop and even the flies seemed to have left the kitchen door. When children cry they are handed a box of Kleenex, so much for a motherly touch.

Every now and then it seems I stumble across something from the past that I feel is worth remembering. Some things that at the time were just a part of our every day living but very much in tune with the way we lived. Looking back now in deep thought, I realize some of these memories are truly priceless. These were everyday things that have been handed down to us for centuries. Nothing reminds me more of home and a way of life as it used to be than walking into a nice warm kitchen and finding someone's mother in the kitchen wearing an apron.

There is an old saying, "Clothes Don't Make A Man"
Maybe so, but I cannot help but feel, "It Takes An Apron To Make A Mother."

102

The

Barn Sparrow

The Barn Sparrow

As children we all loved birds, pretty well any bird as long as it had feathers. A few day old birds without any feathers on do not look so cute. What boy has not found a baby bird and brought it to the house to mother. This of course is mother's worst nightmare. My mom with 4 kids to look after didn't really appreciate a baby bird in the kitchen. Most often the bird I found would be a baby barn sparrow.

I say barn sparrow as years ago on the farm that was what we called them, and in the city they called them house sparrows. However they are of one variety and officially called the House Sparrow. As little birds they constantly fell out of the nest and to little boys were very appealing and ever so helpless. Once in your hand they seemed to hunker down and hope for the best. Nature maybe told them it is better to get picked up by a human than one of those dreadful four-legged furry critters wandering about.

Perhaps no other bird is loved and hated more then the sparrow. They are cute, friendly, noisy and unsanitary. It seems they can't be one without the other.

When I was a boy we had sparrows by the thousands on the farm all because every farmer's barnyard had a big old wheat straw stack, sitting smack in the centre. This made a perfect place for the sparrow to nest. Hundreds of deep tunnels were rounded out into the stack and made into a nest, lined with twigs and grass and finally feathers. All this was woven together to hold the nest in place.

The sparrow mates for life. The female sparrow usually lays 4 eggs and then starts to sit to incubate them. Incubation time last only 12 days and in a little over two weeks later the little birds will fly from the nest. Sparrows can have up to 4 broods of little ones in a year. Talk about mass production!

When the first white people came to America there were no real, what we call pest birds today, as there were no real buildings to be found for birds to live in. All native birds lived on the ground or in cliffs or trees.

Because our pioneer forefathers were used to having sparrows and a number of other birds living close around them they introduced the sparrow first to New York City in 1850 and then to Quebec City in 1868. The common house or (barn sparrow) then is not a native bird, but rather a British species that was introduced to North America. This is the reason we always hear it referred to as an English Sparrow, when actually it is not a sparrow at all but a European Weaver Finch.

When the first sparrows arrived in America there was little natural winter food for them as the sparrow needs farm agriculture to survive. Fortunately this species had learned over hundreds of years how to survive when the going got rough.

There were no cars at that time so everyone used horses. These horses were often pampered and well fed. Wherever the horse dung was dropped you would find the sparrows picking through the dung for whatever grain feed the horse had been fed. Today we call this recycling. You see the sparrow was away ahead of us. Thus the sparrow followed man and animals closely as together they emigrated west and north across the country.

Wherever you found man and horses, barns and sheds and houses you would find sparrows. It is without a doubt the world's best-adapted bird to human settlements.

Given a chance it seemed most sparrows would choose the straw stack to nest, but others would build anywhere in the open, places like under an eave in an open shed or verandah. Once they decide to build a nest they are very stubborn about getting on with it. You can destroy the nest time and time again and they will keep putting it back together again. It is more a test of wills, man against a little bird.

My grandpa was an Englishman and it seems most English were used to eating game meat. It could be duck, deer, rabbit, pigeon, and oh yes, sparrow. My grandfather liked sparrow pie.

He taught me how to catch them by the hundreds very easily. He would take a steel hoop off a wooden barrel and stitch a large burlap bran sack onto the hoop. Then he put a long pole across the hoop and tied it fast.

After sunset when the sparrows had gone to bed for the night we went out to the straw stack. With lightning speed we smacked the pole against the stack and chances are each time we did this a dozen sparrows would take flight. Of course they flew into the sack and fell to the bottom into a churning screaming tangled mass of feathers. After a few times you would have more than enough for a number of sparrow meat pies. I don't remember ever sticking around to watch what happened to the sparrows. I myself never had the heart to eat them.

The sparrow likes to be outdoors flying about the buildings, but during the winter he likes to fly into the upper part of the barn. It is a spacious area out of the wind and snow and fairly safe. It is also a place where there was always some food to be found. Often an open granary door could be very inviting, but they had to be wary of the barn cats as they were always watching for a chance to catch them. They often flew in flocks as if they felt there was safety in numbers. After all, in a flock of a 100 sparrows against one cat what were your chances of getting caught?

Up on our farm we had many barn cats. They were not pampered cats like the cats we have around us today. These were working cats. That is, we had cats because we needed them in and around the building to catch rats, mice and birds and thus protect our granaries. Other than the morning and evening ritual of gathering around the skim milk pail in the cream separating room the cats were on their own. They were never fed an ounce of anything except to let them have all the skim milk they could hold. Mind you, some could hold a lot of skim milk. They sat by the pail and lapped and lapped until they looked like floating balloons.

Of all the cats we owned the best-loved one was "Ole Chummy" a large cinnamon mother cat, full and overflowing with love. When she sang she just about burst and slobbered all over you. She was also an old vagabond as she loved all the neighbourhood toms and thus raised us 2 and sometimes 3 litters of kittens every year. When she didn't have kittens to feed she still felt the need to hunt. Old Chummy thought there was no better way to show us how much she loved us than drop a fresh, but very dead sparrow at your feet.

My mom especially appreciated it, because there was one less sparrow stealing her hen feed.

Wherever a sparrow goes it seems it has to poop upon landing and again as it goes to leave. This is what has made it a very unwelcome guest on many farms and around many homes. During those days when we had sparrows by the thousands because of the straw stacks we could not touch anything in the barn or sheds and not get soiled. Wherever there is bird poop there is always great danger of diseases and parasites, perhaps even more today than years ago.

Over the last number of years the farmers have changed from mixed farming to cash crops. This meant no more straw stacks in the barnyard. This would lead to fewer nest sites and fewer broods of sparrows per year. Then gradually the old barns were torn down and the sparrow was forced to leave and find a new home.

Without a doubt there are a lot fewer sparrows down on the farm today. Those that are left have turned to houses and outer buildings to find a safe haven. Many are now in the cities where they find people with bird feeders willing to feed them. They may be small but they are very aggressive and get their share by chasing other birds away.

All this was many years ago in the past and now I am retired and live in the city. I have a nice condo with a balcony and a number of flower boxes and flower pots. I also have a large beautiful male Ocicat cat called Mandy. Mandy likes to spend time out on the balcony all summer and even in the winter watching the birds. The sparrows flutter onto the wide wrought iron railing just to tease her, but he sits there patiently and bides his time. Some day down the road ……well I will tell you about that.

One day last fall I had left him out on the balcony while I was hard at work on my computer. Suddenly my computer mouse went flying off the board and under the desk and then there was a scuffle at my feet. I looked under and there was Mandy all wound up in my computer wires and cables. I didn't realize what was going on but I chased him out of there and then left the room for lunch.

A short time later Mandy came rushing through the kitchen as if to let me know something really exciting was going on and I should come and see. I followed him into the den and found him sitting in my computer chair watching a beautiful full-grown sparrow flutter up and down the den window hoping to get outside.

Apparently he had caught the sparrow out on the balcony and without hurting it he brought it in for me to see. As I never noticed him come into the den he let the bird go free at my feet and then tried to recapture it. That was why he got all tangled up in the cords at my feet.

I rescued it and cupped it in my hands. As in days of old it hunkered down in my hand as if it knew it was a lot safer to be in the hands of a human than to take chances with one of those four-legged furry critters. They are really scary.

It was a beautiful bird and appeared not hurt in any way. There was not a mark on it, so after I showed Mandy's catch off to Fred and Muriel my neighbours I took it out to the balcony and let it go.

The last time I saw it, it was dipping and diving flying south.

The Starling

110

The Starling

When I was very, very young --- that's a long time ago, I would say in the mid 1930's, I remember my dad pointing out a strange bird in the barnyard to his dad.

His dad of course was my grandpa. They had never seen a bird like this one around the yard before. It was a dark chunky bird about the size of a robin with a short tail and a longer than average bill. It had a dull black coat and a few spots around the neck. It was anything but pretty. Later we found out the starling moulted in the fall and that when winter came its coat changed to a shiny black with oil like multi-colours on the neck and chest. If it was not for its chunkiness one might say it turns into a beautiful bird for a few months of the year.

Other neighbours started to see this new bird in their yard and around their barn too, and in time dad found out the new bird was called a Starling. Of course at first most people enjoyed the thought of a new bird species added to the many they already had. My grandfather referred to them as "Teddy Boys" after the boys of his youth in England. They strutted about in their new shiny winter plumage.

Being that they were by far in the minority of the local birds we could not help but admire their spunk and aggressiveness. However as time went by we learned that someone had opened a Pandora's box. They robbed and killed, tantalized and invaded and fouled up the neighbourhood. The harmony in and around the barnyard had disappeared. No bird was safe, nor could they live in peace again.

Over the next few years we watched in amazement as the Starlings multiplied at an amazing rate and became an aggressive cruel pest like no other birds in North America.

The Europeans had brought the Starlings to America because they missed the birds of home. It was one of the most foolish and misguided deeds they did to their new homeland. Now we are faced with a pest from coast to coast we cannot control. It was in the early 1890's that they were released in New York City, and now there are multi-millions from New York to California and north in Alberta all the way to Fort McMurray. Where there are people and buildings there are Starlings.

As a small boy one of my jobs was to, "Go get the mail".

The mail was delivered 6 days a week (yes that's right 6 days a week) to the mailbox some distance out the lane at the Mitchell Road. It was one of those large old-fashioned mailboxes with a drop down door on the front. The door had a letter opening near the top cut into it about an inch and a half high by five inches wide. It was apparently just right for a Starling. Everyday they filled our mailbox with a mixture of coarse weeds and hay and straw, and 6 days a week I had to rescue the newspaper before they trashed it. If the paper got messed up it was not pleasant to handle. This went on day after day, year after year. Ok, ok, ask me now, if I like Starlings!

I don't know why my dad didn't figure out a way to stop it, but he didn't. I guess the way he figured it was he had a boy for the job so why worry about it.

After the rain you will see the Starlings enjoying a bath in the water puddles in the middle of the yard. They have a gala time as they thoroughly enjoy bathing usually along with several others of their kin. Even when the Starlings have a brood of wee ones back home at the nest, they seems not to have a care in this world. They are very much forward, always strutting their stuff and are on the take and fear nothing. Life to them is forever joyful as they exchange gossip and playfully mimic other birds.

When looking for a place to nest they will take all the choice sites and drive the other birds away. They are not above biding their time while another bird builds a nest and then they move in and eat the eggs and reconstruct the nest to their liking.

Starlings have two broods a year with four to five eggs laid in the nest at a time.
The eggs are a pale greenish blue and incubate in twelve days. The birds are able to leave the nest in about 25 days. It is believed they manage to average about 8 birds a year. Once the growing fledglings leave the nest they usually join with other flocks of juveniles and go mess up the neighbourhood like spoiled teenagers.

When I had my Barber Shop in a plaza in South London there were about two inches of space left over the long store signs and the roof from one end of the plaza to the other. The sparrows took over this area to nest. Several of the tenants were avid bird lovers and were blind to the problem it created. There were the usual businesses in the plaza, my Barber Shop and a Beauty Shop along with a restaurant and cake shop, a Mac's Milk and a few others.

While the sparrows were building their nest they dropped grass and straw and bird dirt on the sidewalk below in front of the stores. Every morning I had to go out there to sweep it up because when the customers walked in it they brought it into the shop on their shoes. However most of the shop owners didn't seem to mind a bit. Of course they were the ones who didn't seem to own a broom either.

Once the baby birds started to hatch the Starlings would arrive thinking this was a smorgasbord made just for them. The early morning air was filled with the sounds of birds fighting and screaming as the Starlings tore the baby birds from their nest and ate them right in front of their mothers. The sight was gruesome and the sound of the screaming birds drove my early morning customers crazy. They walked into my Barbershop shaking their heads saying, "Jack it's a good job you're deaf, so you don't listen to all that".

Yes, I was deaf so I could not hear the fighting, but I could still see naked baby birds lying on the sidewalk and many being dismembered by the Starlings. The sparrows in turn hopelessly attacked or tried to distract to protect their wee one but it was always too late. As the Sparrow has 3 and 4 broods per year it was party time everyday for the Starlings and especially first thing in the mornings.

After watching this go on for several years and making no headway with the local shop owners to end it, I decided I had to do something on my own. I called the city health authorities to come out and see. They in turn contacted the landlord and told him he had to stop the nesting over the sign. It all ended very quickly.

My neighbours were not at all happy with me. A couple even came to my shop and were very angry with me. They asked me why I didn't love little birds.

The landlord did a beautiful job of filling in the space over the sign, but sadly there were a lot of unhappy sparrows flying up there flapping their wings, wanting to get back in to nest. No doubt there were a few baby birds left behind to starve. This bothered some of the shop owners to no end. They stood there shedding tears for the poor little birds, so one night someone tore off a stretch of the new material to let the mother birds back in. The next day the landlord had it fixed right away and a notice was given to all the shop owners that this was called vandalism and if anyone was caught they would be charged.

This brought a new quietness and cleanliness to the plaza and the birds left to find a new home. In time the neighbours forgave me as the problem went away.

When nesting around the farm, that is the barn and outside shed buildings, the Starlings favoured any kind of hole on the outside of the barn to enter and build a nest. They didn't seem to prefer being on the inside of the barn. Often it would be in behind a loose board on the side of the barn where hay or straw was still packed against the boards. This was ideal. A loose board under an eave of a shed was also excellent. If there was a chimney on the house you were not using, that too was a brilliant place for them to build a nice warm nest. Many people would start up their old fireplace at Christmas time or in a cold spell and get smoked out of the house until they cleared the nest the Starlings built.

It may not have been a very wise choice but they used to nest inside the down drainpipe from the eaves trough of both the barn and the house. This clogged up the drainpipe and was more a nuisance than anything else.

I believe when the Starlings first came to our farm they stayed around all winter. There were very cold hard winters in the thirties with many feet of snow. Often I would look up at the old house chimney where the wood or coal furnace smoke was rising into the air. Huddled all around the edge of the brick chimney and atop the cap of brick taking in the smoke and heat would be a number of cold, cold looking Starlings.

Today it seems the modern Starlings gather in flocks of thousands and move to the city at night to a special roost site. While they will do this they are not a true migrating bird. They are smart enough to know that it is warmer in the city than in the country on a very cold night and also they can find a place out of the wind.

Besides their aggressive nature they are also noted for their ravenous appetites. In the spring they will strip your cherry tree of cherries the day before you're ready to pick them. Then all summer they stick around mainly for the meat --- that is they live on insects. They eat cutworms, beetles, grasshoppers, ants, bees, wasps, spiders and earthworms and everything from salamanders to household garbage. That is the good news, but in the fall they turn to fruit such as apples and grapes.

I wish there was something good I could say about the Starlings but knowing the bird as I do I feel it is nothing more then a pest, a pest which we will have to learn to live with as they have no known enemies and are resistant to diseases. While a cat might catch and kill one they won't eat them for some reason, and I know it's not a guilty conscience.
Before you invite them to your feeder you should know that the acid in their feces will corrode stone masonry and metal. You should also be aware that there are some very bad bacteria and parasites in their feces, which pose a health risk.

I am deaf now and cannot hear the sound of their singing, but no doubt there was a time when I was young, I heard them sing. I cannot for the life of me remember the sound. I have heard though, many people do enjoy their singing.

"They too …had their own low whisper songs. Though with them it was scarcely song at all, but low, musical ejaculations and gurgling notes, and from time to time, as though some of the gossip had passed, some bird would break in with a kind of ironic whistle, high, clear and oh so sweet." by - David Grayson

When Credit

Was

Your Good Name

"When Credit Was Your Good Name"

Years ago, honesty was a common virtue within our community. It was a way of life that we had all learned to live by. Growing up at Motherwell I thought that honesty existed everywhere. It was in my neighbour's homes, in our local village and throughout our community and my home town.

We loved, respected and trusted all of our neighbours. It was much later in life that I remember once telling a friend that I really never met a dishonest person until I came to the big city. I am not proud to tell you this but when I first ventured into the city I got taken more than once. Simply put, my country trust was not appropriate for life in the big city.

There was a time when your family name was who you really were. You could seal a deal on a handshake and take it to the bank. You see there was no such thing as a credit card. You yourself were your own credit. All you would ever have throughout your whole life was your good name, and it was up to you and no one else to honour that handshake and thus protect that good name.
Out in the middle of the country there were many village stores who ran their businesses on credit. Most farmers didn't always have the cash for their daily needs. The country General Store owner knew that Mr. Smith or Mr. Cooke had to have their tobacco or they might be grumpy all day, so give them credit.

They also knew Mrs. Smith and Mrs. Cooke needed certain things to bake food for the family. I never really heard of anyone being refused when they said those famous words, "Just put it on my bill." These stores let you run a floating credit bill within reason. When it started to get what they thought was too high they picked a quiet time when the store was empty to mention that very soon you would have to do something about your bill.

I marvel now that they were able to stay in business, but the reason they did had all to do with your good name. They knew who you were and you were aware that your good credit depended on you straightening up that bill.

Wherever you went locally all you had to do was to mention your family name, and that is who you were. Your good name had been earned before you were born by your parents, and their good name earned for them by their parents. If your family ever got a bad name it was very hard, if not nearly impossible to earn it back.
In my case all I had to say was, "I'm Jack Cooke the son of John and Reta Cooke" and I was as good as gold, all because both my dad and mom had lived up to their good name and I was made very aware I was expected to live up to it also.

We learned early in life honesty was the best policy.

Time moved on and it seemed as if true trust and honesty crossed a fuzzy line and to many of the new generation today it is unclear. Some even came to believe that old saying, "There is a fool born every minute, and one to take him".

I am afraid as we get older it is easier to become that fool so we find ourselves often being targeted as such. However every now and then something good happens to give us hope, so do not despair.

There are still a lot of good people out there but the problem is that an honest or a good deed seldom makes the morning paper.

It's sad but bad news always gets the larger print.

The Hired Man

The Hired Man

Alonzo was a hired man; perhaps it was a choice he had made for himself. Thus rather than take on the responsibilities of running his own place he would rather work for others. In a way I guess he was lucky, as many hired men in those early years had nothing of their own except a few clothes in a battered old suitcase. Alonzo did have a place to call home. Thus when the time came and he wanted to be on his own, to rest and renew himself he could always go home.

The place he called home was already a run down grass farm long before I first remembered meeting him. It was a farm he inherited from his parents. I have no idea how the farm came to be so run down, but every year one could see it was slowly self-destructing. The handsome old white brick house stood solid but unkempt as the cattle pastured up to its door.

Perhaps the farm fell into disrepair during the years of the great depression and then things just lingered on and on while the barn crumbled into the ground and the fences for lack of repairs disappeared into the earth. I remember it as a rolling grass farm with a few anchor posts dotting the area from the road front to the hardwood maple bush at the rear. As a grass farm, what it had going for itself was a beautiful stream of ever flowing water a short distance beyond the crumbling barn.

I cannot remember just when Alonzo came into our lives and became our hired man, but I am sure it was right after my grandfather passed away in 1941. Dad had polio in 1930 and for the rest of his life he had a bad leg that caused him to walk with a limp; so if he was going to farm he needed someone to help him at times.

I don't remember what kind of wages Alonzo was paid. I don't think it was a lot, but it seemed he was satisfied and dad and Alonzo got along just fine.

In those days almost everyone smoked. So if you were a smoker it was good to have a boss who smoked too. I remember the many times I watched dad and Alonzo each with a cigarette spending time chatting while the work was put on hold. I think that was one of the reasons Alonzo enjoyed working with dad. "Lots of smoking time." Every working man expected to get paid while on a smoke break. At that time it was just one of those unwritten laws. I also think Alonzo liked to work for dad as he never felt pushed to work any harder than his comfortable gait that was never all too fast. He and dad just worked at a steady pace and got the job done. Then of course there was my mom's good cooking at every meal, I know that counted a lot. All week long he was always assured of a clean bed and three good meals a day and then sometimes mom would send something home with him for the weekend. It was about as good as it got for a hired man.

On Saturday nights he always went into town with us and headed straight for the Hicks House, the famous old bar in midtown Mitchell. It was there he would meet with many of his old drinking friends.

People used to go to town on Saturday night for an outing, a social evening to shop and meet your neighbours and friends. The sidewalk was full of chatting, gossiping friendly folks catching up on all the latest news, but we would not see Alonzo on the street all evening. About the time the movie was out and we were ready to go home along would come Alonzo smelling just a bit pickled but in a happy mood. We would drop him off at his lonely gate and say good night and continue on home. He would enter his lane through the barbed wire gate and walk up the grassy lane towards the old dark brick house.

He was fairly dependable so as a rule early Monday morning he would turn up, broke, and ready for yet another week's work. It was almost as if he hadn't left. I don't remember giving him or receiving from him a friendly greeting.

In fact I never felt that he really cared that much for me. Many times when my dad chastened me for something I had or had not done he would add his voice of disapproval in support. This did not go over well with me. On the other hand my sisters could do no wrong and he would always take their side against me.
That was not good, as we all know sisters are not always right. Ouch?

He worked for us for many years, in a way one might say, "With The Seasons," always going and coming on his own. When he didn't turn up for work one day dad was not alarmed. After a couple of days dad checked with a few of the neighbours to see if anyone had seen him. No one had seen him for several days. Dad thought he better go to his house on the old farm and check on him. He found him dead on the couch in the kitchen. I am not sure just what he died from. I don't remember that he had any health problems so perhaps it was not a bad way to go.

There are times that I think of him and his life as a hired man. At that time I was too young to give it all much thought. As he was in his own community he was better off than many hired men who more or less drifted from one place to another.

Dad never had another hired man, as by this time I was able to do the work. For dad this was good as a son is expected to work for, "pocket spending money."

Many years later I went to Western Canada and became a hired man myself. I was fortunate to have some very wonderful bosses who were good to work for.

Yet I cannot help but believe that behind every hired farm hand there is a better man trying to get out. Hard work never hurt anyone, and working for someone else can teach you many things including patience, skills and empathy, so down the road you may become a better person, but unless your able to move on from being, just a hired man, all that may not happen.

At the end of the day, at the end of the week, at the end of the month or season what did most hired men really have to show for all their year's work?
Very few ended up with more than last week's wages.
At the end of the year the hired man on a farm has nothing
of his own to look backward at with pride,
and nothing to look forward to with hope.

My inner self kept telling me this was not for me as this was indeed a dead end job, a job I should break free from and get on with a life of my own.

Alonzo was the only long time hired man we ever had, but during the thirties we did have a number of men drift in for a short time. Some stayed overnight and some for a few days and then just walked off down the road. Often they dropped in just before suppertime asking for work and a meal and then would sneak off like a wounded animal after dark.

I myself was named after a young lad from north central Manitoba who spent the summer and winter on our farm. He was a very young and very homesick lad. He came to the farm in the summer of 1928 before I was born and asked to help with the harvest. My dad and my grandpa took pity on him and hired him more because he was just a homeless kid than anything else. They learned to like him.

When the harvest was off dad and mom didn't have the heart to turn him out on the road to nowhere so they told him he could stay the winter and do chores along with dad and grandpa. He was a good kid and they learned to love him.

His name was Laverne Burgoyne. On October the 17, 1928 I was born and christened Jack Laverne Cooke. The following spring dad and mom talked the lad into taking the train home. I remember hearing my mom say he did write a few letters after he got home. In 1928 Manitoba was a long ways away and we lost track of him. I've always been curious about him and I would have liked to have met him.

We all understand a lot better today than we did when much of this happened so long ago. Now it is written in our history books, but for better or worse I lived it. Many of these drifters called tramps were just someone's sons. Unfortunately many had no farm skills and were not much help on the farm. They were just on the road between cities with no job and no money and an empty tummy. They came from a place where there were no jobs and they were heading to a place where there were no jobs. There was neither a lot of patience nor a lot of understanding of the big picture of what was going on with the country at that time.

Few could afford newspapers and there were few radios and no TV.

It was a time when you were fortunate to live on a farm.

We understand a lot better today than we did when much of this happened so long ago.

The

River

126

The Thames River

The Bridge Over The Thames at Motherwell, Ontario 2007

The River had always been there long before the white man and the settlers. The Indians and early trappers founded the pathways along its shores going north and south. The settlers used the same pathways for a time in those early days to travel. From its source to its mouth it is about 273 km. or about 150 miles long.

Everything started from the river and then slowly ventured out into the surrounding bush lands. When the first settlers ventured into the country away from the river there were few roads or trails to follow. If you were looking for a place to settle, then near the river's crossing was the place to be. It was the place to build a general supply store or a blacksmith shop, the basics needs of every village. Once the farmers and families arrived it would become the hub of the community.

One of the first things the early settlers had to do was to build a church and a school. Since the river was at the heart of the community it was there that the first school and church would be built in the valley or on the bank of the river.

For over a hundred years this tranquil setting of a village by the river in the valley came to be dear to our hearts. Over the years hundreds of children from the surrounding area went to church and school in this village by the river. Many left and went out into the world to succeed in distant places, but when you ask them where is home and where did they come from, they would always say they came from Motherwell, that village in the valley by the river Thames.

In my thoughts it is hard to separate the village without thinking of the river. I like to think that there are many like myself who every now and then wander north along the river "Thames" and to the village "Motherwell" and sit a spell and think of those yester-years when all was well in Motherwell.

It is then we realize how much our world has changed. The village itself is all but vacant and in ill repair. The ever green pastoral setting along the riverbank is no more. The cows that once kept the riverbank grazed as a meadow and free of underbrush have long gone. The river that once dominated life in the community is now but a tormented meandering riverbed with a pittance of water struggling to find its way amid grassy islands and wild brush.

Memories linger of better times when laughing children roamed the village street on their noon hour or after school was out, buying 5 or 10 cents worth of candy, or a chocolate bar at the store, walking past the blacksmith shop, listening to the hammer on the anvil - a steady powerful blow, sometimes venturing within the doors to watch the bellows blowing on the coals, making them glow.

Then my mind wanders back to the bridge and I see Keith and Jack lying on the rods as we called them, one on each side patiently trying to snare suckers in the shaded water below. The water is clear and I see the limestone riverbed below. I hear the rumble of a car or truck as it passes over the bridge breaking the quietness up and down the valley.

In the summer many of the boys would want to go swimming or fishing in the Thames River on the way home from school. Without a written note from your parents this was a no, no. If the teacher caught you she would send you home and the next morning you might get called to the front of her desk and asked to explain yourself. She left no doubts in your mind and in the minds of all your friends you had sinned.

I remember the day after school when a half dozen boys decided to go swimming in the Thames River south of the Motherwell Bridge just before the rapids. We were <u>more or less</u> out of sight, except for a spot at the very west end of the bridge.

South of Motherwell Village at The Rapids

We were all frolicking in the water having a great time when some one shouted, *"There's the* teacher." Six nude boys streaked ashore, dressed in great haste and made fast tracks for home. I bet the teacher chuckled over that one for years, but as they say, "Boys will be boys."

Then there were times in the winter when the teacher allowed us to take our sleighs or toboggan down to the riverbank on our noon hour to play. It was on such an occasion that I got a broken arm. I had a rather cumbersome hand-made sleigh, one that my dad had made to haul bags of feed to the barn from the road, when our lane was blocked with snow. I had just started down the hill when a faster toboggan rammed my sled and made it change course. There had been an old lime kiln dug into the hillside at one time many years ago and my sleigh dove over it and from there it was more or less a shear drop onto the river ice.

Somehow I landed with my arm twisted behind me and I was in a lot of pain. The kids gathered around and sort of rolled me onto my sleigh and pulled me back up hill all the way back to the school. The teacher came down to the boy's coatroom and tried to take a look at my arm. However it seemed my arm had somehow jackknifed inside my leather jacket sleeve. Try as they might they could not get my arm out of the sleeve. My Aunt Maude in Detroit had given this jacket to me. It had been her son's until he outgrew it and it was now my prized possession, and I could see it was in great danger as the teacher approached me with a pair of scissors.

My teacher took the large shears and began cutting up the sleeves and I screamed and bellowed with all my might and she thought I was in great pain. My pain was not so much from my broken arm as it was from having my leather jacket sleeve cut up. None the less the teacher didn't realize that until many years later.

Winter and The Old Steel Bridge at Motherwell

In the winter the river froze very deep. Sometimes the ice was 12 inches thick, thus it was very safe for us to skate on. There were skating parties on dark nights when lanterns were placed on the ice for us to see to skate by. It's great to be young as somehow it seemed we never really got cold as long as we kept moving.

Spring would come and one day the ice would crack and start to move, often jamming the river and backing up for miles. Then suddenly it would break free. At times it would cause floods and vast property damage for miles up river, even taking out some of the township bridges.

When I was very young I remember standing on the bridge with my grandfather looking down into the water. There was a huge limestone abutment holding up the bridge in mid-centre of the river. The abutment was interfering with the torrential flow of the water and it made a deep whirlpool perhaps 10 feet deep where it split the water. I can remember the pull as I looked into the whirlpool and I leaned forward without realizing it until my grandfather's hand was on my shoulder.

Standing there on the bridge I could feel the reverberations of the present and the past colliding, the ice crashing on the stone. It was like living a piece of history.

In time the water would recede and the flow would be back to normal again. It seemed it was a normal occurrence for people who lived in the valley by the river.

Year's later the Thames would be tamed by a series of dams controlling the flow, yet deep within my mind I remember it as a river unrestrained, and unpredictable a source of power. It held us in awe, and in fear, yet in admiration.

Trafalgar Bridge   By Jack L Cooke 2007

I remember those evenings after a hot day's work at harvest time when one of the neighbour boys would come by to see if I would go to the river for a swim to cool off. Many times we would go to Trafalgar Bridge on the Thames, a few miles south of Motherwell. There was a deep hole under the bridge, which made it more interesting. Mothers worried about their kids though as it was rumoured that some boys dove off the bridge into the river. That was dangerous as there were a few great rocks down there under the water the size of a kitchen stove. Of course we promised our mothers we would never do a thing like that. Whatever, as you know most boys have very poor memories, and a lot less common sense.

Then there were Sunday dips at the mouth of Black Creek, where the creek flowed into the Thames north of Motherwell and south of the village of Fullarton. A huge rock lay just under the surface of the water in the mouth of the creek where it enters the river. From this rock we could dive into the water. This is a special place for me as it was there that I first realized I could swim. On a nice Sunday there would be an assortment of guys there from Motherwell and Fullarton, all neighbours and friends and we had a great time.

As far as the fishing went I was never a fisherman. The few fish I did catch my mom would not cook. There is nothing so uplifting as bringing home what you thought was a trophy fish and your mom squealed and held her nose and kept telling you to throw the thing out. We seldom ate fish as neither mom nor dad would ever clean a whole fish. Thus I am not a fish eater today. To me there is nothing so disgusting as seeing a whole fish lying on a platter. Don't get me wrong, I do love fish as long as they are free and in water and able to swim.

> So here I am once more in the village in the valley by the River Thames
> Contemplating the past --
> I like to remember -
>
> The sound of the bell over the door at the village store.
> The pride they took in well-kept lawns and flowerbeds.
> Those long summer days when the river flowed on and on
> - quietly from the north to the south.
>
> I like to remember the water bouncing gently over the rapids south of the bridge and then flowing on into what we called The Bay. From there it flow gently on to the Trafalgar Bridge. In my mind I can still see the farmer's cattle contentedly pasturing on the riverbanks and drinking water in the shallows.
>
> The sun sets behind the river's bank to the west
> A lone crane flies in and settles down upstream to the north.
> Down by the bay the boys are fishing.
>
> When summer comes again I will take yet another trip north
> To the village Motherwell in the valley by the River Thames.
> Trying to recapture that which I lost.
> Today it seems, but like a dream
> A dream I once thought would last forever

The Motherwell Village and Area Homes

The Andrew Watson House

The old Barr Homestead

Motherwell …… As I Remember It

The Bert Brown House

The Old Steel Bridge

The Motherwell Store

The Blacksmith Shop

134

My Dad's Cars

1925 Model T Ford

My Grandfather never drove a car. In fact he never drove a tractor. If it had a motor on it he simply crashed. He knew it had to be far beyond his know-how. The only thing he ever drove with a wheel on it was a wheelbarrow, a wagon and a buggy. I know that sounds rather backward. Yet in a way he was just like so many of our seniors today and the way they look at the computer. They simply crash.

Until 1925 there were no wheels in the family. They drove a buggy all summer and a cutter all winter. Instead of shining the car on weekends they brushed down what they called the "driver," which was their faster horse. Now don't get me wrong, I do love horses. In fact so much so I drive a Mustang today. It is the second one I have owned. I guess I should explain to you though that my Mustang doesn't have hooves, but it does have some very nice wheels.

In 1925 my grandparents were 59 and 60 years old respectively. The long buggy rides they had once enjoyed so much and so often in their youth, were now wearing them down. They sometimes drove all the way from the farm at Motherwell to Woodstock to see my grandmother's sisters. It was a distance of about 60 miles one-way. They would leave the farm early in the morning and enjoy a quiet scenic drive through the countryside. They would stay overnight and come home the next day. Now in their sixties the long drive was just too much, and especially so for my grandma. They would arrive home late in the evening dusty, exhausted and worn out. Each time they would say that it was their last long trip.

At the time my dad was 26 years old and courting my mother and like all young men of that day, he was in great need of a car -----or so he thought.
In fact he was so sure he played t his little game up to his dad and said,
"Just think if we had a car I could drive the 60 miles down to Woodstock in less than two hours at the outrageous speed of 30 miles an hour. Why we could slip down and back the same day, and you would have more time to visit and yet we would be home for chores by 6 or 7 o'clock. You would not even be tired."

He managed to sell this idea to his dad and get a brand new 1925 Model T Ford. This was the very first car in the family and while grandpa had paid for it he had no idea of driving it. Grandpa looked at a car as just transportation. He well knew one could love a horse but how could anyone love a car!

Dad however was not home free yet as grandpa owned the car and he had his own ideas about what was right or wrong for a car. To him it was about common sense.

One evening they arrived home from a trip down to Woodstock and back all in the same day. The evening milking was done along with the rest of the chores. My dad though wanted to court my mom that evening so he got all duded up and headed out to the car. He started it up and was about to back it out of the driving shed when my grandfather stopped him. Grandpa told him to take the driver and the buggy as the car had enough for one day. With that he threw the buffalo robe over the hood and patted it on the hood and said, "LET IT REST."

As every one knows the model T was a great car and dad drove it into the 1930's.
Somewhere about 1934 he bought a newer but second hand 1932 Model A and drove it for a number of years. My best memories of it were when on one of those mornings when for some reason we were going to be late for school my mom offered to drive us. When she did this we would often pick up some of the kids who were walking, as one could not just pass them by. They would all joyfully pile into the car one on top of the other -- Joyce, Stanley, Oliver, Helen, Anna and Vernon. We were all good friends then and shall remain ----- friends forever.

Dad's 1932 Model A

They soon learned however when they got out of the car not to stand around at the rear of the car as my mom would let out the clutch and the tires would spin and throw dirt, gravel and stones at them. It was embarrassing to hear them say,
"Run she's gonna let out the clutch."
For some reason mom just never seemed to remember to let that clutch out easy and so the car lurched forward with a bunny hop and the wheels spun and shot gravel. That was my mom.

Mom denied this to all her grandchildren but I am telling you right now, it is true.
"Grandma had a heavy foot".

One day in the mid 1930's perhaps about 1935 my dad came home from town driving a very splashy special second hand car. It was called a Durant. It was a luxury car and what they called a touring car. It was I think a 1933 or 1934.model. My mom flipped and was very angry with him, and when my mom was unhappy the whole family was unhappy. She had no idea he was even thinking of trading cars.

The truth was when my dad left home to drive to Mitchell he had no idea of buying a car either. It was just a case of falling in love with the car. That is something my mom would never understand.

The car had been for sale at Jack Edmonds in Mitchell and poor dad fell for it right off the bat. He had always dreamed of owning a Durant and was afraid if he didn't buy it on the spot someone else would and he would miss out on a golden opportunity. It was in a two-tone royal blue and had upholstery one would die for. It had storage bags on the inside of each of the four doors and also on the back of the two front seats. There were lots and lots of cigarette trays and cubbyholes. Under the front seats there were hot water heaters to give heat to those who sat in the back. There were two great headlamps one on each front fender and a tire in a casing mounted right inside each fender.

How could mom not love this car?

The 1933 or 1934 Durant

Little is remembered about "The Durant" cars today. In fact it is forgotten.

Yet I feel Durant cars deserve a place in car heaven and a place in car history.

William Durant was born in Boston in 1861. He quit school and went to Flint Michigan to work in his uncle's lumberyard. Michigan and especially Detroit for some reason became an industrial hub of America. First it was the manufacturing of the horse carriage and then along came the motorcar.

In 1885 Durant began building horse carriages and by 1890 he was the largest carriage maker in America. In 1904 Durant was asked by Buick to join their company as general manager. In 3 year's time Buick was out-selling all other car manufacturers in America and Durant was made President of the Buick branch of GM.

Durant was interested in car racing and for prestige reasons joined a French team. It was through his love for car racing he met Louis Chevrolet.

The two became fast friends and joined forces to design a new car. Durant was not a mechanic. He just liked to design the carriage. This worked out well with Chevrolet and in 1921 they put together their first car. They called it a "Durant Touring Car". It was a great success. They were the first cars to use a six-cylinder motor in 1928.

In spite of all his great success, history was about to deal Durant a hard blow.

First the stock market crashed in 1929, followed by the great depression. Money dried up and no one could afford to buy a large luxury car. In the fall of 1933 the last Durant car was made, a 1934 model. Then the company was bankrupt.

Knowing all this now I expect my dad had followed Durant's car history and always wanted one of his cars. So when this opportunity turned up he just had to take it, or he would never own a Durant one of the world's truly great touring cars.

However how does one explain all this to my mom? My mom had very much a common sense approach to cars. Her motto may well have been,
"If it isn't broke don't fix it." - - or trade it.

To my mom any car was just a car, nothing more. It was transportation to get you from one place to another. As long as the wheels were still going around why on earth do men always want to trade cars?

I remember the Durant as a prestige car to ride about in, and the ride was far better than any car I ever rode in. Dad had a number of small problems with the car but in those years it seemed every make of car had problems. It was expected. However in this case the manufacturer was bankrupt. So in the end dad decided not to keep the car too long as he might have trouble getting parts for it. Besides mom had not forgiven him for buying such a luxury car. She saw no need for it.

Somewhere around 1938 my dad bought a 1934 two door V 8 Ford. It was what they called a coach. It came with a tire on the rear trunk door, and was in a nice medium shade of green. I think of all the cars my dad ever owned I liked that car the best. He drove that car hard and for many miles. Dad was a good but a fast driver, nevertheless I can't remember hearing my mom ask him to slow down.

Dad's - 1934 Ford V 8

My sisters and I would sit in the back seat terrified, hanging on for dear life as my dad took the corners of the Mitchell road on two wheels. Coarse gravel would shoot up banging the underside of the fenders, and then be thrown madly out from under the rear tires. Behind us he left mile after mile of dust billowing in the air only to eventually settle on the neighbour's fields.

He was always in great haste to get to wherever it was he was going. On the other hand when he got there he was never in a hurry to leave. Mom and we kids would sit in the car and wait and wait and wait for him while he chatted on and on with ease. It was as if there was no one and nothing more important in this world than he himself and the topic of the day. Nothing could hurry him, absolutely nothing. That is until he was behind the wheel again. Then the dust would fly and the gravel would shoot all the way home.

Many times when I could have gone into town with the family I begged off to stay home, because I had this crazy idea it was best that cars use all four wheels.

We entered World War 2 in September of 1939 and thus no more cars were built until 1946. The manufacturers were busy turning out jeeps and tanks and all kinds of military equipment plus airplanes and, oh yes, guns.

As the war lingered on people began to buy up the better used cars, as no one wanted to end up with an older heap that would not work. In 1940 or 41 dad traded the 34 Ford in for a black 1938 Ford V 8 a very fast speedy car. Its worst feature was that it had cable brakes and leaf springs on the front as well as the back. This meant that it rode a bit like a board, and did not have a very cushion-like ride. Henry Ford was very stubborn about this and kept the leaf springs on the front end of his Ford cars until 1939. All other cars already had hydraulic shocks in front.

There was a problem with cable brakes. They either worked or didn't work. When they worked you could stop on a dime but the cables stretched and at times one would be tighter than the other. Thus you could not stop or not stop straight. They would grab the disc and drums hard and wear everything out fast. They continuously had to be adjusted. Other than that it was a good working car.

1938 Ford V 8

One of the first things dad had Jack Edmonds do was to weld the flimsy Ford grill back together and then give it a brand new paint job. Then it looked just like new.

Dad drove that car for a number of years. We had several very hard winters and deep, deep snows. Many of those years you could drive all the way to Mitchell and never see anything but the road straight ahead of you. It is hard to imagine this now but the snow was piled up on both sides of the road to the telephone lines in places. On the average it was 3 cars high in height. I am talking about 12 and 15-foot snow banks for miles on end along the road.

My dad would put car chains on the rear wheels and leave for town. He was fearless. The roads were not kept open as they are today, so many times he would have to buck a lot of snow all the way into town and then buck it again to get back home. There were times when the cross-drifts were as high as the hood and dad would floor the gas petal and hit drifts at full speed. The car would hit with a bone-jarring jolt and you found yourself bracing against the forward throw. Then the chains would dig down to the frozen gravel and we would fly forward again.

As we approached the next cross-drift it seemed for a time we were all but airborne until the rear wheel's chains dug down and once more took hold and we lurched and ground steadily ahead. Often when he did this he broke a link in the set of car chains and there would be a terrible racket under the fender. We clang, clang, clanged ahead, the broken chain links hitting the under side of the fender.

It was at times like this that I found out my father knew a foreign language of many four-letter words. My mom would look at him shake her head and bite her tongue. Many times this would happen when he was dressed up, or when it was very cold so he would not get out of the car to fix the chain. He would drive all the way into town and back home with that darn chain clanging all the way. It drove me nuts. Usually everyone carried what they called a roll of black wire and a pair of pliers in the truck to fix chains. Along with the scoop shovel it was common winter equipment. I cannot imagine these things happening to my Mustang.

In 1944, I got my beginner's license and was able to drive my dad's car. I am sure he was thrilled at the idea. Still I remember that day dad let me drive his car.

"One day in Mitchell as we were getting into the car my dad handed me the car keys saying I could drive home. Mom got into the back seat along with my three sisters and dad took the passenger side seat.

I had watched dad shift gears on a standard gearshift all my young years so I had that down pat in my mind. I did very well and I think my dad was impressed. Soon we were well out of town and on the road home. I was cautiously travelling maybe 30 or 35 miles an hour and my mom kept shouting,
"Slow down, slow down," I think she was just a might bit nervous. Now that is hard to understand as my dad took all corners on two wheels and she never complained."*
* From the book – "Getting By In A Silent World"   by Jack L Cooke

That summer our Young Peoples were going to Grand Bend for a picnic and swim. I managed to get my dad to let me drive his car. My three sisters and Ruth and Norma Nairn were going with me. Ruth knew a short cut it seemed through Kirkton and on west. Very soon I was approaching a long low very narrow cement bridge. I entered the end to drive across and about the same time a car entered from the other end. Now this bridge I guess was made for horse and buggies and not for cars. It was soon evident that we could not pass. I went to apply those cable brakes and not much happened. The car kept moving ahead and I did a slow crunch into the front end of the oncoming car. His bumper entered my dad's car grill. My poor dad's newly fixed grill took it badly and disengaged. I too was very crushed, as that night when I drove the car home I had to explain all this to dad. Dad was very understanding about it and I was very much surprised. However it was only a few days later that he took me into Sawyer's Garage in Mitchell and pointed out a 1939 Plymouth coupe he wanted me to have, but that's another story.

During the war years there were many cold stormy nights that my dad would leave home to drive our next-door neighbour Bill Roger back to the Air Force Base east of St Thomas. Often it was quite late and a night when no one should be out on the road. Nevertheless "Duty Calls" and there was nothing dad liked better than the thrill and adventure of going out on a stormy night. One of the neighbour boys, Bill Morrison would sometimes go with him. They left prepared, dressed in warm clothes and rubber boots and took a couple of snow shovels along with them. It seems everyone had confidence with dad's driving and his Ford car. The next day I would hear wild tales of how high and long the snowdrifts were and how fast he hit them. It was of course always amazing.

Then in 1946 my sister Laurine was in Normal School (Teachers College) in Stratford and on weekends she would want to come home. No I don't think it was me that she missed, so I wonder if it could have been Oliver the boy friend. On many Sunday nights Bill Morison our next-door neighbour would go with dad bucking snow across country to get Laurine back to Stratford for school on Monday morning. They always made it but had some great tales to tell later on.

At the time I believed all that they told me, but it seemed the snow was always deeper and the drifts wider and longer when I was not with them.

Dad drove that 1938 Ford all through the war years and it served him well. By the mid to late 1940's you could almost see through it as it was rusted out everywhere. I don't know what was holding it together. Still it could take the corners on two wheels and buck snow like nothing else. In the end he traded it for a black 1946 two door Chevrolet. That was one of the very first cars that came out after the war. The 1946 Chevrolet was an excellent car loved by all those who owned them. My dad included.

The 1946 Chevrolet

I always remember when Alex (Sandy) Morrison bought one of the first new 1946 Chevrolet cars that I saw after the war. I thought it was truly a dream car and at the time far beyond what I would ever be able to afford. We found it hard to believe that he had paid a whole one thousand dollars for a car. That was an amazing amount of money in 1946. Little did Alex or anyone else realize at the time it would turn out to be one of the best investments he would ever make.

Canada, a nation of unemployed workers and wandering hobos, entered World War Two in 1939 and five years later in 1945 it came out of that war an industrialized nation. However as a country we were in debt up to our ears but even so no one seemed to understand this kind of debt nor did they seem to care.

We had for the first time a kind of hope, born of peace and some kind of prosperity we never experienced before. We also had a bad case of inflation and as you know they say inflation is bad for you, but it was inflation that bought our way out of our national war debts and gave us for the first time in our lives real prosperity.

You see wages increased, as did the value of our money and everything we owned. Our farms, our houses all increased in value, the factory workers were paid more money and the farmer got more money for all the farm products he sold. Canada paid off its war debt with inflated money.

As for Alex -: Five years later Alex's 1946 Chevrolet was worth as much as he had paid for it or even a wee bit more. Trust me, I know, as in the late 1940's my dad and I both bought Chevrolets ---- dad a 1946 and me a 1947.

I like to remember that year when dad and mom took a trip to Western Canada with my mom's brother and wife my Uncle Roy and Aunt Myrtle Butson. My dad parked his 1946 Chevrolet in the driving shed and told me not to touch it. That was not a problem, as I liked my own car better then his. So it sat there in the driving shed for six weeks gathering dust and pigeon poop.

At this time my youngest sister Jean was being courted by Billy Butler. Bill had just found a nice black two door 1946 Chevrolet exactly like my dad's.
Imagine what my dad thought when he arrived home from the west and saw what he thought was his car parked up by the house when it should have been in the driving shed where he left it. He lit into me right off saying,
"The last thing I told you when I left was not to drive my car."
Poor dad, he never did like to eat crow.

Dad drove that car until the late 1950's and traded it for one of the nicest looking cars he ever owned - a two-tone robin's egg blue and white 1956 Pontiac. It sported white wall tires and a huge chrome bumper and grill up front. There were also two chrome stripes down the white hood.

It was a beauty and the kind of car that even my mom could like.

1956 Pontiac

In the spring of 1961 dad and mom sold the old farm on the Mitchell Road at Motherwell. They moved in with my youngest sister Jean and her husband Bill Butler for a short time until they had time to decide, what to do. You see the chance of a quick sale came up unexpectedly. Now they had to make a decision.

My dad found steady work driving tractors out on the farms at Motherwell and mom found she was left alone in town as both Bill and Jean were at work.

Eventually, mom told dad if he wanted to be out in the country all the time then they should find a small place and move back out until they were ready to retire. They found a small farm for sale on the Mitchell Road just south of the Village of Fullarton, so they bought it and lived happily there from 1961 to 1969. It had a fantastic square cut fieldstone house with an attached garage for the car and a nice little barn.

They parked the '65 Pontiac in this small tight garage, which at one time had been a part of the attached summer kitchen. It was built entirely of stone and attached to the stone house. For some reason these stone walls sweated continuously and the car was always wet as if it had been left out in the rain. One day when I was home visiting I was shocked to see how much rust was on the car. I begged dad to leave the car outside where the air would circulate around it, as the garage was too wet and rusting his car. Dad was not easily convinced but in time he found that when he left the door open his car was not quite so wet. Thus in time the car spent more time parked outside.

In 1969 they decided it was time to finally retire and to move to Mitchell. They sold the farm making a very good profit and bought a nice new little place on Arthur Street on the east side of Mitchell. This was mom's first new house and she was very happy. On the other hand my dad went shopping for a car and bought a 1968 sand or gold coloured 4 door Chevrolet Malibu.

Whenever I bought a new car I always remember how happy my dad would be for me. He would walk around it making some nice comments and then ask for the keys so he could take it for a drive. This memory is dear to my heart to this day. On the other hand my mom showed little interest or approval of any of my cars.

1968 Chevrolet Impala

Years later I remember visiting one of my sisters whose son had just bought an expensive new sport car. I asked her what she thought of her son's new sport car.

She said. "Oh I have never really taken a look at it."

I told her about the happy memories I had of my dad because he took an interest in each and every car I ever bought and then how my mom never showed any interest at all in my investment and that was not nice. I said,

"Even if it kills you get out there and tell him how nice the car looks and ask if he will take you for a drive. Remember every new car he will ever own will be a big deal to him, so share his happiness and years from now he will remember you for that … kindly."

Dad and Mom bought a nice pull type trailer that matched the colour of the car. They travelled all over Ontario and a few trips to Western Canada. It seemed that mom was never happier than she was when they pulled out of their driveway and onto the highway with the trailer. I remember she told me once how much she loved travelling and camping out in the trailer somewhere afar off where they had never been before and then she said,

"And do you know the good part is coming back home to my new little house."

They had several winters in Florida in the trailer.

In the end they sold it to a cousin, Ivan and Betty Lou Norris.

Then they bought a 23-foot motor home and took to the road in earnest.

Dad's very last car

My dad's last car was a brand new 1978 gold-coloured four door Grand Plymouth. It was the first brand new car he ever bought. Although it was new it was what they call a year-end car. He bought it in the spring of 1979.

I like to think that those years were very happy ones for them. They were comfortably retired and living in their new home. They had a new car parked in the garage and a motor home in the driveway.
However when I think of it now I feel sad that mom had no interest in cars and she didn't want to go with dad to look at cars. I don't think she ever helped him to pick out a car. In those days a lady didn't go wheeling and dealing buying a car.

Nevertheless in the spring of 1979 when he came home with the same coloured car as he had traded in my mom was not at all happy.

Dad's 1978 Plymouth Grand Fury

Dad never had anything more then a fender bender in all the years he drove a car. He was a good driver although in his younger days he drove far far too fast. I did note he was taking great precaution in his later years. He was aware his reflexes and eyesight were failing.

At 82 years old he drove the motor home all the way to Alberta and home again. My sisters and I were very worried about him, and also very proud of him.

Dad continued to drive but only in Mitchell and to visit friends close by.
He also made it a point to get home before dark. Yes, he did all the right things but we were still worried something bad might happen to them or someone else.

In 1984 they decided it was time to sell the little house, and again move on.

"They moved into Ritz Villa, one of Mitchell's finest retirement homes. It took a while to adjust and settle in, but it seemed they decided to make the best of it. Dad still had his wheels and that alone meant a lot to him. There were a few bad winters and dad just let the car sit on the Ritz Villa lot all winter. When he did drive he was good about not driving at night as his eyesight was failing him.

I am sorry to say we sort of tricked him out of his driving license in the end, as we wanted him off the road before something bad happened. His birthday was Oct. 21st and his driver's license was due for renewal on that date. We said,

"Well since you don't care about driving on winter roads why don't you take a six month license and save money?" That appealed to dad. He thought that might be a good idea. However the next spring when he wanted to renew his license, he could not drive the car to Stratford to renew and that was just as we had planned it.

My sisters had told me not to give in to him if he asked me to drive him to Stratford. Sure enough one fine spring day he asked me to drive him, and he was very angry with me when I said I could not do it. He left the room in a huff and did not come back until I was ready to go home. As I walked out the door of their apartment I said,

"I will see you in a couple weeks."

Dad said, "Well we will be here, where else would we be? We can't go anywhere"

It wasn't funny for him, but I have chuckled over that many times over the years.

He got a fair price for his Grand Fury Plymouth car selling it right off the Ritz Villa lot and this seemed to help him to forget the pain of being without his wheels for the first time since 1925."

To my Dad's credit is the fact that in all his years of driving he never had anything worse then a fender bender in the line of an accident. I marvel at this, as it was well known he had a heavy foot, and on the old gravel Mitchell Road he would kick up miles of dust and rounded all those corners on two wheels.

Finding

Happiness

Finding Happiness

It is said, "Happiness is the Journey, not the destination".

However if you find happiness at the end of your journey, you have been twice blessed.

Growing up on a farm in the great depression, gave us the basic ingredients one has to have to find happiness. There is a time in your life when it is better to have less than too much. Everyone has heard the old saying, "What you have never had, you will never miss" and I am sure it is true. You don't have to have everything to be happy, if so then you learn to appreciate better what you do have.

Perhaps one of the worst things parents do for children today is to see that they have everything, just to be sure they have as much as everyone else's children.
They grow up with big expectations; if they receive less they will not be happy.

Growing up in the thirties we had to make do with whatever came our way. Even though we grew up with no store-bought toys I don't remember being bored or unhappy. We didn't look to toys to find amusement. We had to find our own interests and make our own entertainment and I believe our lives were enriched because of it. We found our happiness in many ways. One was our great old farm dog that greeted us every morning with a wagging his body from head to tail and endured our many hugs. We also had a dozen or so barn cats that practically stood in line at the kitchen door to be petted. We checked out the litters of little pigs and played with the calves. There was even Pecky our dear old one-eyed pet hen who also came to the kitchen door and demanded her share of our attention. We swung on the swing and climbed the old apple trees. We checked out my mom's large vegetable garden for great looking bugs and explored my mother's many flowerbeds for new blossoms of the day. Everyday brought something new into our lives.

At the time I didn't really understand the nature of the happiness that I had found. I feel I understand it better today. Happiness came to us from within. It was largely attitude. We found that by giving something of ourselves we received happiness in return. Happiness was from the heart and very simple and didn't cost anyone a cent. The greater part of your happiness depends on your attitude and your disposition and not your circumstances.

When you hug a loving dog his body virtually vibrates with joy from head to tail and the happiness you gave it, comes back to you. Thus your incline to hug him again and yet again. When you pet a cat it will purr and sing. Thus happiness comes back to you. When you plant a garden you will watch the garden grow and the flowers bloom. Happiness comes back to you. When you meet you neighbour or a friend greet him cheerfully.

Happiness is like an echo, what you give out comes back to you.

There is an old Chinese proverb that says, "Happiness comes over the shoulder when you are not seeking it, or expecting it". It comes to you unaware. If you directly aim at it, you might drive it away and be forever without it.

Happiness is a natural experience and yet so many cannot seem to find it.

Every now and then we need to take time to reflect on the meaning of our own happiness. It is a feeling of personal well being, of satisfaction, and of gratitude.

I believe we should lean heavily on the gratitude.

Happiness is something that should vibrate from us; thus we share it with others. It's hard to be happy if you keep it all within. The purring of your cat tells you it is happy. Your dog will come to you wagging his tail telling you he is happy. Who can put his hands on a happy dog or cat and not feel the radiation of its love and happiness? People show happiness in many ways. They suddenly do acts of kindness. Their faces light up with smiles, and their laughter comes easily.

Happiness also comes to us when we can see the needs of others and not get too wrapped up in ourselves. It is there that most people lose their happiness.

I am troubled that the emphasis in many churches seems to be in obtaining personal happiness and peace through <u>their</u> church and <u>their</u> religion. I feel the emphasis should be on getting right with God and with fellow men and women. I have a very dear old friend who goes to church everyday to pray, and I do mean "EVERY DAY". She is so dedicated to her church she has no time for friends.

In that respect I have found that some that do not lay claim to any profound belief at all often put the rest of us to shame. They are always there if you need them.

Being deaf I have always been very much aware that all things in life are not equal. However it took most of my life to understand that there are many people who on the surface seem to have everything and yet they lack that something that separates the soul from the body. Just take a look at the rich and famous people we know in the world today. They spend all of their time chasing after happiness yet all the time squander the good life they were given.

My First Barber Chair

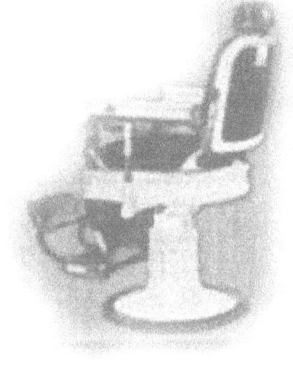

While deafness took its toll and shaped my life I would not let it take me down.
I know I have been blessed as I have found a certain amount of happiness and real contentment within my barbering career.

It seems that over the years I became acquainted to hundreds and hundreds of people and when I go about South London I almost always bump into a face I know.

In retirement I have also taken to the computer like a duck in the water, and thus I now have wrote two large books.

I bought a new Kodak lens, and I am getting is enjoyment and new. If that something is time and a lot of patients. working on the patients. how helps. I am

camera 5.0 mega pixels with a 10X optical zoom some great picture like those in this book. There happiness in the challenge of doing something just beyond your grasp, then go for it. It will take Being retire I have a lot of the former and I keep Having a good friend with a bit of camera know improving and I will get there in time.

You will find that we always have enough of whatever it takes to be happy if we are enjoying what we do, and what we have, and not worrying about what we can't do and don't have.

Happiness comes to us not so much by doing what we like, but rather liking what we do.

I still cut hair one day a week. It is a special few who are not ready to give me up. Some arrive carrying a cup of Tim Hortons coffee and a muffin. Life now is in the slow lane so we have lots of time to chat.

I find happiness working in my flower garden and the 8 huge flowerpots I planted last spring, plus all the flowers on my balcony.

Then every night Mandy my cat sits on my lap and purrs contentedly.

You cannot buy your happiness,
Cause happiness is free.
Don't you know, or can't you guess,
It is there for you and me.
by George Savige

Old Farm

Water Wells

Water and The Farm Well

My grandfather once told me that there were two things a man should do in his lifetime - plant a tree and dig a well - thus leaving something behind for those who follow you. I am happy to say I have done both. I planted a tree and dug a well.

Water was always very important to the pioneers and especially to the farmer, as he not only had to have water for the house but also for his livestock. A hundred and fifty years ago the ideal solution to be assured of a good supply of water was to build your house and barn near a river or an ever-flowing creek.

Most of those early wells dug near a river or creek were not very deep. The water from the river or creek simply filtered its way through the soil into the well.
The soil itself was not contaminated in those days and was a good filter and made the water pure enough to drink. For many years this worked without any problems. These shallow wells quite often had wood cribbing to hold the sides from caving in. The earth that was taken out of the well was leveled around the site to elevate the level of the soil so the runoff from the surrounding area would not enter the well from the top, but rather seep in by sinking down through the soil.

There were always problems with debris and frogs getting into the well and wherever there are frogs you will find the odd snake that enjoys a frog for lunch.

Our old farm had two wells that I sort of grew up with. One was behind the summer kitchen at the house and the other behind the barn snuggled against the gangway.

Both wells were less than 20 ft deep and encased with large fieldstones. The fieldstones were placed in a circle with care. Each stone as it was put in place overlapped the two below. There was no doubt about it; most of these old stone wells were built with great skill. Over the years I had to go down both our wells to clean them out when the water got low. I did that by bracing my feet against the stone wall and descending slowly, balancing myself against the water pipe. Now that I am older I would say it was not a very wise thing to do, for if one stone came loose I might have ended up at the bottom of the well with other stones falling on my head.

There were two other well sites on the farm that I knew the location of. Both had been hand dug and abandoned many years before my time. One was by the gate at the rear of the 60 acres that opened onto the 11th. Line. The other was at the rear of the 100 acres and for years had been used as a dump site. Each had been covered with logs that were rotting and falling into the well. Every now and then dad threw a few old logs or cedar posts on top to keep the cattle from falling in. I believe these were shallow wells as each had been dug in a low area where they would fill with water each spring. Naturally, as kids we played around, and over them, just as our parents had warned us not to. I noted they each had rotted wood siding.

There are few things more mystifying than an old abandoned dug well and especially those encased with stone. Every foot of earth was removed with hour after hour of labour and sweat, then every stone put in place with precise care. Every old well has a story locked away that could be told. As I have dug a well I know people do not dig a well without a reason and then in the end abandon it.

An Old Abandoned Stone Well

* There were a number of years in the dry 1930's when our barn well would go dry both in the winter and summer. When this happened we had to draw water from the house well to the barn. Hauling water in the winter is a miserable cold job and in the summer, time-consuming as there are many other things we had to do.
We used two large wood barrels on a stone boat to haul water.

"I remember that grandpa had a long down-drain pipe like the ones, which came down from the eave troughs on the corner of the house or barn. He attached the elbow over the pump spout and the other end into the barrel. It worked well. When grandpa got tired pumping I took over for a while, and sometimes we both pumped together. When we had both barrels full we draped a burlap sack over the top of the barrel and then dropped a

barrel hoop over each to hold the water from slopping out over the top. This worked well. We usually kept a third horse around for small jobs as the team might be in need in other places. Older, more or less retired horses earned their keep doing these kinds of odd jobs. In our case first it was old Frank then old Doll that got the job. Two barrels of water were a heavy pull for an old horse." *

- *From the book, "Getting By In A Silent World" by Jack L Cooke*

In their lifetime these many farm wells throughout the country continued to pump out excellent water for over a century. There were always dry years when the water table across the country was down. Usually it was followed by years when everyone managed to get by, but now our well water was in serious trouble.

Hindsight as they say is often crystal clear, but at that time no one was paying much attention to what was happening to their ground water. Nearly 100 percent of the farms at that time were stock farms. They raised beef, dairy cattle and pigs.

Over the winter, a huge pile of manure was stored in the barnyard. It was commonly called, "The manure pile". The rain and snow came down on it and by spring the barnyard surrounding the manure pile was full of liquid brown water, running off into the fields. This water was seeping down into the soil and eventually got into the well. We first noticed it when the water started to look like tea and frothing on the top. In spite of this we continued to use the water for our stock. I think dad hoped the problem might go away, but each year it got worse.

It was in the fall of the early 1950's that we made the decision to dig a well. The fall plowing was finished and the weather was right for hard work. Somewhere I have read that it is best not to wait until you are thirsty to dig a well.

The first real wells were all dug by hand using a short-handled shovel, a pick and a crowbar. The size of the well depends a lot on the size of the guy digging it, as he has to have room enough to swing his pick and use a shovel. As a rule a hand dug well is wider at the top and gets a bit narrower as it descends.

Of course the easiest digging is always the first few feet. Once you get down a short way you would hit clay, rocks and sometimes gravel. Then the fun begins.

How deep you have to go to reach water depends on the water table and the lay of the land in your area. On our old farm all the dug wells were under 20 feet.

After a few feet the guy doing the digging descends down the well on a ladder. Once he is down in the well the ladder is pulled up so he has space to work.

A rope is lowered down the well with a bucket on its end. Every time the bucket is full of earth and rock the guy down the well shouts to the guy above "Ready" and stands back against the wall in case the bucket should fall.

As a rule a sort of winch is set up to wind the rope and bring the bucket up.

It was not without danger as in some kinds of soil a well can cave in. Digging in heavy clay though is usually considered very safe for wells 25 or 30 feet. Still I remember the feeling of standing deep within a well swinging a pick and wielding the shovel. There is an uneasy eerie feeling of constant danger, of being out of place or somewhere unnatural. I cannot say I enjoyed it but when my dad asked me to climb a ladder or go down a well I did it because I was asked.

A few days after dad decided we needed a new well he went to visit one of our neighbours. His name was Cotton Harmer. It was said he had found water for many farmers in the area by witching for water. I almost fell off my chair when my dad told me about this.

This was something I was going to have to see before I would believe it.

Cotton was a good neighbour and I hated for him to see that I did not believe in well witching. He arrived in a dusty well-worn truck the very next day. He had brought along a heavy piece of what we called number 9 wire with him. It was the kind of wire the farmer used to put braces on brace posts at each end of the 40-rod field.

He bent the wire into the shape of a U with about 6 inches of wire sticking out on each side to use as a handhold. He held the U wire at arm's length in front of him and began to walk across the yard. The U wire began to turn in a circle and he followed it to the well behind the house. He said that this was the spring the house well was on.

Then we went out behind the barn and walked back into the first field but nothing happened so we went down the lane to the second field. Just as he entered the gateway the wire began to go crazy and spin wild. He stopped and walked left and right and he told dad there were two very strong runs of water that joined right there. He pointed right in the centre of the gateway,

Cotton turned to me and said, "Now do you believe me?"

I still was looking for some logical reason as to how it was done. At the time I was a very strong lad of about 20. Cotton took a pair of pliers and made a loop in the one end of the wire, and then he asked me to put my gloved two fingers through the loop and hold the wire from turning. The wire cut into my heavy leather gloves and turned. I had to let it go. Strange as it may seem I know now it works.

My hearing was getting very bad and my world down the well was very quiet.

Down there I found it difficult to know just what dad might say, yet somehow of all the people in this world I understood him the best

It was late in the fall and at the end of the day and I was down about 20 feet. Dad said, "Jack did you hit water?"

I said, "No dad I will level it off and call it a day".

Dad said, "Put the pick back in the same place you were the last time".

So I did and boy was I in for a surprise. A wall of water and sand gushed in from the west side of the well. It tossed my shovel aside like a toy and I shouted to dad

"Send down the pail" --- "I mean the ladder I am going to drown down here".

Finding water at the bottom of your very own well is an awesome experience.

We went for supper and did the evening chores then took the lantern back to the well to see how much water was in it. We could hardly believe it as the water was about a foot from the top. Winter came on and the well sat there full of water. We reasoned that since it was full there was little chance of it caving in. In the spring dad got some steel forms for making round cement tile. I think they were about four feet wide and 30 inches high. Every couple of days or so we would take the form off and put it back together and mix cement and gravel next to the well and make a new tile. I believe we made 8 tiles.

In the spring we had the PUC or Hydro from Mitchell come out with a big pump to pump the water out on the well. They could not shut the pump down, as the water would rise so fast in the well. It flowed like a creek down the laneway. With a hoist above the well they lowered the first tile down. Then dad sent me down the well to try to make it sit level. The hydro pump was trying to keep the water down but the force of the water on the west side of the well was blasting in sand and water. It came with such force it sent my shovel flying. I was also very afraid the hole would enlarge and cause the well to cave in. It was a scary experience and I could not level the tile. So they decided to just lower the rest of the tile down on top of it hoping the weight of 8 tiles would cause it to level itself.

The last tile went in sticking up about 18 inches above the ground.
It sloped forever to the southeast.

At that time we finally went modern and bought an electric powered Durra well pump. Thus we finally had lots of water in the barn. The water was good and abundant and it lasted us until dad sold the farm to Aaron Penner in 1961.

The Penners eventually gave up livestock farming for cash crop and caged layer hens. When they built a large building for broiler chickens they drilled a deep well to boost their water supply.

There were many wells on the old farm; some served for a short time and others were there for many years. There was a time when this country used to be proud to say air and water were free. It is sad that we have abused both.

An Old Wooden Windmill
"You never miss the water until the well goes dry."

Monday

Is

Washday

Monday is Washday

As a kid I always hated Mondays. Monday was the day my mom went from room to room gathering up all the dirty or even slightly soiled clothes to wash.

It was done religiously. There may be seven days in a week, but God only made one of them to do the wash. As long as we kids were at home, come hell or high water, on Mondays my mom did the wash.

The earliest visions I have of mom doing the wash were with 2 galvanized steel tubs and a washboard in the middle of the old farmhouse "summer kitchen".

Almost all large brick farmhouses had a built-on area that they called a summer kitchen. The idea being that during the winter people lived in the main part of the house because it was warmer, being built of double brick and having a furnace in the cellar under it. (No one used the word basement in those days)

The summer kitchen was built of single brick with windows and doors on both sides. We also had a verandah front and back. As people had to use wood cook-stoves all summer long to cook their meals, the kitchen would get hot. Having a summer kitchen with cross ventilation made sense … as it was cooler.

My folks however had a bigger problem. You see my grandfather owned the farm so they had to share the house. Mom and dad got the summer kitchen to live in year round and one huge cold upstairs' bedroom over the unheated dining room was shared by all of us. All summer we were very hot and all winter we were very cold.

In the winter when mom did the wash in the kitchen there was no way for us to escape it. We were right there in the middle of all the action …….. four little preschool age kids amid several piles of laundry two tubs of water a scrub board and a roaring wood fire in the kitchen stove. However did mom keep her sanity?

Both tubs would be a little over half full of water. The one tub had hot water in it and the other tub had cold rinse water.

The scrub board was a sheet of ribbed galvanized steel or sometimes it was made of ribbed plate glass enclosed in a wooden frame. The sides descended at the bottom beyond the ribbed scrub board to the bottom of the tub acting as legs. At the top there was a small shelf on which was placed a bar of strong yellow lye soap. The bar of soap was dipped into the water and then rubbed over the ribbed board to apply the soap and then followed quickly by the clothes. Mom would use her knuckles to add pressure to cleanse the clothes. Each time she finished washing something she had to wring the water out and place it in the rinse water. After washing a number of things she hand rinsed everything in that rinse water and then wrung it all out by hand and put it in a wicker clothesbasket. Long before she was done her knuckles and hands were red and raw. This was every Monday so she had six days to heal.

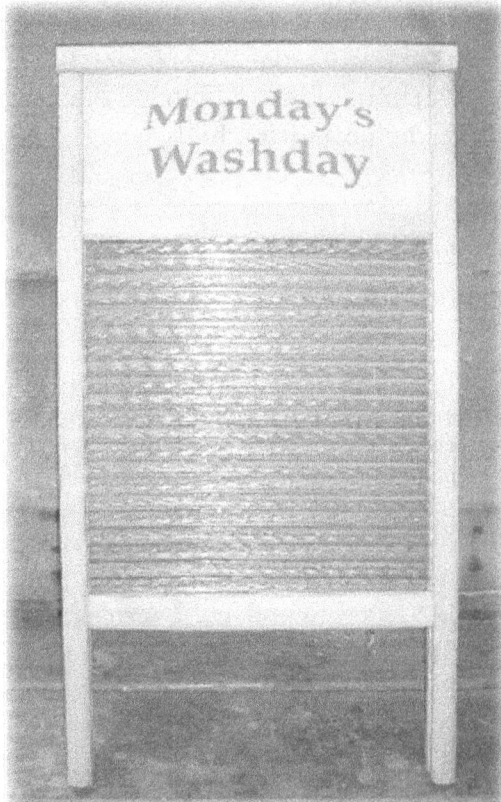

On the floor all around were piles and piles of clothing. My dad's bibbed overalls loaded with all the natural elements found in and around the stable were in one pile along with all other really dirty clothes. Then there were piles of whites and piles of coloured clothing such as bedding and towels and then my mom's and my three sisters' clothing and my own.

I found that my mom washed anything that looked as if it had been off the hook or hanger.
All this fussiness added hours to her workload but it had to be done.

There would be a copper boiler for water on the stove and a healthy roaring wood fire beneath heating it even if it was mid summer. How else does one get hot water? Cold-water soaps would not be invented for many years yet.

The secret to doing as much wash possible with the minimum amount of hot water was to use the water three times over. Do a white wash first followed by a coloured and then my dad's bibbed overalls. After my dad's bibbed overalls were done the water went out back from the woodshed door where it left a greasy trail.

You're going to ask me how come I know all this. Well you see on washday you had to sit and sit and wait and wait for your dinner. The kitchen table would be under siege. There was everything from wicker baskets of wash waiting to be hung on the line to soaps and blues and whatnots. Then the stove was being used to heat boilers of water. Our world stood still on Mondays until the wash got done even though I was starving for dinner. Now do you understand why I hated Mondays?

I know my dad was aware just how hard all this was for mom, as he would sometimes come in from whatever he was doing on cold winter days to hang the clothes on the line for her. Dad however never did learn how to hang clothes on the line just right so as to please my mom. Why sometimes he faced the side with the patches on toward the road. She was most often quite embarrassed about his style. Mom wondered what the neighbours would think and dad thought as long the clothes got hung and they dried who cared. It was elementary.

While I was still quite young I remember when my dad bought mom a gas powered washing machine with a swinging ringer on it. Mom was in heaven. Now she washed everything she could lay her hands on. I know I was the whitest kid in the community. You may think I am kidding but it is true as mom dressed me in white shirts and white pants along with white socks and white shoes. There was a time everything I owned was Rinso white and stiffly starched. I was expected to stay that way, clean, but as you know boys don't have much fun staying clean.

As I grew older I would often hang the wash on the line for my mom in the wintertime. I tried to do it with a fair amount of style so mom would not complain.

When the temperature hits about 30 below F hanging clothes can be a brutal job. First you can't hang clothes with gloves on, as you have to use clothespins. At first there is some comfort in the wicker basket of freshly washed warm clothing as it is warm on your hands to the touch. Now you must be careful about touching the clothesline, as your damp fingers will freeze instantly when you touch the wire.

You lift your damp warm long johns out of the basket and fold the shoulder area over the wire and push down on a clothespin. By the time you get the second pin in on the other shoulder you will note the long johns are almost frozen stiff. Putting your hand on the long johns' shoulder you push out the line and reach for the next piece of the wash. By the time the basket is half empty you note that in the stiff cold morning breeze the long johns and dad's bibbed overalls are frozen stiff. They have now risen in the air and are jerking up and down in the breeze all the while pointing due north to the true north strong and free.

It seems at times when the weather is just right clothing will freeze dry and at other times the wash remains stiff as a board all day. By night mom would say those hated words, "Jack, go bring in the wash."

Our clothesline was off the west end of our verandah and reached high into the old maple tree at the far end to the west. As you wheel in the line you reach for the clothespins and begrudgingly they give up the clothes. Each piece of clothing is still frozen solid to the line, so with your bare fingers you pry up the frozen cloth inch by inch setting it free.

Each piece of clothing is stiff as a board and you lay it over the wicker clothesbasket and crunch it down. You will be lucky if you can get the smallest line of clothing into the basket as frozen clothes take up a lot of space.

When you finally get them all off the line your fingers are so numb you're hardly able to fold your hand let alone open the kitchen door to get back in the house. Once inside your frozen hands will now start to pain as they thaw out. It is very painful. Never mind you have until next Monday to heal.

Now there was an interesting fact about travelling over those country roads on a Monday so many years ago. By watching the clotheslines you could tell a lot about the family that lived there as you drove on by. Some lines had many men's clothing on while others had smaller boy's on it. Still others had lots of girl's clothing on it large or small. Some clothes were ragged and well on the way of being worn out and some lines were mostly new. The clothesline told a lot about the number of family members men and women, boys and girls and their wealth and their style as a family. So no wonder my mom worried about putting on a good show when our clothes were hung out on the line.

When my dad and mom retired to their little house in Mitchell they bought a new side-by-side washer and dryer and it took a lot of work out of washday.

However old habits are hard to break. On nice days and sometimes some not so nice days mom would insist on hanging her clothes out on her back yard clothesline. She always claimed the clothes were more fresh and soft.

In their later years I tried to visit my dad and mom every other week.

But never on Mondays.

The Mailman

The Mailman

In every community there are what we call unsung Heroes. They are people who served their community diligently, dutifully, year after year without fanfare. While they are with us it might seem that they were simply doing their job. After they are gone we miss them and it is then that we realize while you can hire someone to do the job you can't hire dedication. People like this are few and far between. Such a man was our mailman Bill Pelling who served us many years ago six days a week. To this I feel I must add that old refrain, come rain, hail, sleet, or snow.

Bill was short in stature but long in dependability. He looked uncomfortable when dressed up in his navy blue suit but he maintained his military veteran posture throughout his lifetime. Like my mom's brother, my Uncle Hugh Butson, he was every inch a veteran and commanded respect as he moved about the community.

Bill lived in the village of Fullarton with his wife Mary (Rogers). I knew him quite well but only as our mailman. He may not have been everyone's friend but everyone who knew him realized he was every inch as honest as he was reliable; he was a man worthy of our trust.

This is what he brought with him into his job as our mailman. To this day whenever I see a mailman I think of Bill Pelling and measure them by his values.

Few people today give any thought as to how our first settlers got their mail in those early days. It was The Canada Company that brought settlers into our area of Fullarton Township. Most of these settlers came from England and Scotland and a few from Germany. When they came they were told they would have a free mail service. Can you imagine a place with no real roads no telephone no radio or TV? Today's generation even find it hard to give up their phones during school hours.

The Canada Company had set up traveller taverns about every twenty miles across Ontario from Hamilton to Goderich. The mail was passed from tavern to tavern each way and eventually found a boat going to England. A letter mailed from a tavern in Mitchell in spring often never arrived at its destination until fall.

However born out of all this was our Royal Mail which earned the people's trust.

Bill Pelling was our mailman long before I was born in 1928. In 1924 he obtained the rural mail delivery for Munro R.R.1, which covered the area around the villages of Munro and Fullarton and as far south as the 12th line south on the Mitchell Road or the road to Motherwell Village. Driving through Motherwell he worked his way back north on the eastside of the Thames River. His route covered almost 30 miles every day.

Bill and Molly Pelling

In 1924 when Bill Pelling first became our mailman a postage stamp on a 1 oz. letter mailed to England, Scotland or Ireland was just 4 cents. To anywhere in Eastern Canada it was 3 cents of which 1 cent was a war tax still left on from the First World War.

This 1cent tax was eventually removed July 1st 1926, when a 1 oz. letter could be mailed again for just 2 cents. Postage continued at 2 cents until 1931 when the 3 cent postage rate was again reintroduced.

The 3 cent postage rate on the first oz. for a letter remained until 1943 when 1 cent was added making it 4 cents to mail a 1 oz. letter.

One of the great privileges we had on our rural route was, if you didn't have a postage stamp to put on your letter you just had to put the three or four cents in a separate envelope and Bill put the stamp on the letter for you. Now that is service.

In those early years he drove a horse and buggy all summer and a horse and cutter in the winter. There were days in the winter when no one should have been out on the road. Yet to no one's surprise the mail was in the mailbox.

One of the problems he had at times was to find the mailbox. We lived on the Mitchell Road, which was a county road. The county had their very own snowplough long before the township. For some reason the guys running the snowplough thought it was fun to clip off mail boxes along the road with the wing on the plough. You could not dig a hole for a new post during the winter as the ground was frozen. So my dad was always carrying out an old board, or two-by- four, and tacking it onto the post. It began to look like a shack. In the spring we would put in a new post and the next winter it would get clipped off again. To solve this problem some people just dug a hole into the snow bank and set the mailbox in place. On snowy days Bill would have to get out of his car and hunt for the mailbox before he could deliver the mail. Yet he never complained.

When conditions got to the place he could not travel by car or cutter he arranged to have the mail delivered down the lines from neighbour to neighbour, each farmer walking through the field to his neighbour, picking up all the mail and taking it home with him. He then called his neighbour to come over to pick it up and pass it on. While this would be quite illegal for us to do today, at that time it worked because everyone knew and trusted his neighbour and no one complained.

In all those years while I was growing up the mail was delivered 6 days a week. In my early years I would find myself watching for his buggy or cutter as he would always arrive at our place about 2 p.m. Later on in the late thirties he delivered the mail using a car all summer and the cutter in the winter.

In 1954 the Munro store and post office burnt down ending its long time service to the community. As the Village of Fullarton had its own post office for many years the mail from Mitchell was now delivered there instead of to Munro.

Bill Pelling continued to deliver our mail until he retired in 1956.
At this time we had to change our address from Munro to R.R. 1 Fullarton.

I have no idea how well Bill Pelling was paid or if he ever had any problems with his job. In those days we never heard of a mailman that went on strike. It was thought he was fortunate to have a government job while others were unemployed.

Still, even today there are people in our lives that to some are invisible. They are there to do their job. Many times I wish I had taken the time to say thank you to Bill Pelling but like many others I took him for granted. I left home shortly after Bill retired but to this day whenever I see a mailman I think kindly of Bill.

In 1924 when Bill started out as our mailman the postage on a letter was 3 cents. When Bill retired in 1954 postage on a letter was only 5 cents.

On January 16th, 2007 the postage rate changed to 52 cents for a 30g letter. However 52 cents today won't buy you the kind of service we got for 4 cents so many years ago. Be sure to cross the T's and dot your I's and don't forget the postal code

The P on the new stamps in 2007 means the stamp it legal until used even if the postal rate increases before you use it. You no longer have to buy one-cent stamps.

Winter and Snow

178

Winter Time and Snow

From The First Timothy Eaton's Catalogue

Being born in 1928 I have many childhood memories of cold snowy winters -winters that started at the end of October and lasted until the end of April. That was a good 6 months of the year. Christmas it seemed, arrived almost halfway through winter. We thought nothing of being snowed in for days at a time. The snowplough was looked at as a gift, a gift that if we were lucky came by once or twice a week. It was then we would get out to town to stock up with groceries.

On the other hand our grandparents spent all winter depending only on the horse-drawn or cutter to take them to town, to church or to the local store. This for them was not a major problem as they had learned to accept winter for what it was. For them it was a time to reflect on last year's bounty, good or bad. It was a time when the world about them grew closer. They took comfort in their local blessings, which was a good community with a school, a church, a solid house, heat such as it was and a good barn where their livestock was warm and secure for the winter. It was a time the family spent more time in the kitchen together.

At times though too much snow could always be a problem even for them. As long as they could manage they would rather pack the snow down under the bobsleigh runners and the horses' hooves than touch it. When it was piled up it only drifted back in deeper with the next storm. So when they walked out the lane they found it best to watch their feet and walk in the area where the sleigh runner had passed over or they would sink deep into the snow. Often kids walked along as kids do, joshing each other, not paying attention to their feet. They tumbled off the solid runner path and walked like drunken sailors stumbling happily along.

The first snowploughing was actually done by local farmers who rigged homemade planks as wings alongside their bobsled and pulled it with a team of horses. Of course

they started out doing their own long lane-ways and then if the snow was not too high they ventured down the side road leading to a main road.
For a while in Fullarton Township it seemed anyone who owned a large truck and able to rig it up to a snowplow was welcomed to join the rest of the local crew.
It wasn't until 1947 that they bought their very own snowplough.

While winter brought a kind of lull to the farm and rural life it was still a season for a different kind of work.

One of those for some people was cutting ice from the river to store in the icehouse for the next summer.

* *"A few farmers had what was called an icebox, which looked a bit like an old fashioned fridge. A block of ice kept the icebox cool. This worked very well, but there was a lot of work involved in getting and keeping ice. In the winter men would go to the Thames River and cut huge blocks of ice. I have seen the ice ten to twelve inches thick on the Thames River. They sawed the ice with special handsaws into twelve-inch squares and called them " Blocks." They lifted the blocks out of the water with great ice prongs and piled then onto bob sleighs. Then with a team of horses drew it home. It would be a very heavy load and the team had to be allowed to stop every now and then to catch their breath.*

The gravel roads were usually snow packed most or all of the winter, so bob sleighs could travel down the road most of the winter without a problem.
Once home the ice was put in what was called an icehouse. When possible the icehouse was built into the side of a hill. Wood sawdust was then shovelled over the ice as it was piled layer by layer. The sawdust was also put down between the blocks so they would not freeze together. Sawdust is a wonderful insulator and the ice would keep in the icehouse all summer."

- From the book, "Getting By In A Silent World" by Jack L Cooke

Winter was also a time for cutting next winter's firewood to heat the house, as firewood needs time to dry. Cutting wood was a skill that every young man had to learn. How many people today can use an axe skillfully and how many know how to use a crosscut saw? Those old timers had it down to a T. The crosscut sailed back and forth across the log as if on a float. The axe landed squarely on the block and the wood chips flew. Good woodcutters earned respect and were always in demand

Our lives changed along with the motorcar and with the demand for open roads.

The roads we enjoy travelling on today have been built up high over the years, allowing most of the winter snow to blow across them. The first roads more or less followed the lay of the land and the snow drifted in from the fence line. The small snowploughs at that time just shoved the snow aside making a pathway down the centre of the road. Every time it was ploughed out it would blow back in higher from the bank that had been thrown up. Later they developed a wing that they could raise up high to wing it back even higher at the top. I remember driving from our farm all the way to Mitchell and never seeing anything but the snow piled high on each side of the road like a topless tunnel. In places it was as high as the telephone lines.

Today we have built up high roads and also huge ploughs that hit the snow and throw it far back into the ditch. Our biggest problem seems to be ice or visibility.

However in spite of all of today's modern advantages of warm homes, warm clothes and warm cars, it seems more and more people do not like the winter.

I wonder. I wonder have the people today turned soft to the very word -- winter.

The people cringe at the very word, it send chills down many people's back.

Snow, that's that white stuff that falls down from the sky making the world around us white. Add the two together and they will either love it or hate it. Believe me, some people just love to hate it. They spend all too much of their time being overly concerned about it. After many years of trying to analyze family and friends and winter I am sure most of this hate is more or less in their heads.

Of course too much cold alone can make our lives very miserable unless we bundle up and that is the secret of enjoying the winter. Dress for it.

That is also why a blanket of snow is Mother Nature's way of protecting everything from your front lawn to the fields of winter wheat, not to mention all those furry critters snuggling comfortably in their burrows. Then there are our trees our shrubs and bulbs. They all depend on a ground cover of snow to survive.

would have no winter wheat for pasta, no maple syrup for pancakes, no orchard fruit like apples for pie and no grapes for jam, jellies or wines. There would be no spring flowers and shrubs such as we have now.

The rewards of having a winter are many, so why do we whine so much about it!

I have often thought that little towns seem to suffer less. If you drive through a well dug out little town in the heart of the snow belt of Ontario in winter you will note high banks of snow neatly piled and driveways that are free of snow. On the other hand in many cities it seems everyone is on their own. No one wants to lay claim to any part of it. You toss it onto your neighbour's lot and he throws it back. The sidewalk ploughs push it out to the curb and the city ploughs it back towards the sidewalk and into your driveway. It is a mad exchange of something no one seems to want. So it's a fact………..

"He who gets ploughed on last gets to keep it."

Then again, children seem to think it's a fun thing.

Have you not watched the simple joy on the faces of little children when they fearlessly climb to the top of a huge pile of snow and slide down or free fall from its top and ---- roll down? It's called "innocence." They are at the age of wonder and pure delight. They haven't learned yet to hate. They live for the moment and right now they are enjoying snow and winter. Never deny your child such delight.

In time they will get cold and return to their heated homes, where once inside they will enjoy the feeling of heat. Once again they are alive. For if you have never really felt cold then you have never really known the joy in the comfort of heat. That is the reason our fireplaces are dear to us. They radiate heat with comfort. The comfort we receive is largely picture-perfect within our mind just as the picture of winter and snow affects us the opposite way. It is largely in the mind.

I have never heard of a child who hated snow, so I feel it is something we learn.
On the other hand
I have never heard of an adult who didn't enjoy a fireplace. It's pure comfort.

As we get older, excesses of almost everything lull our senses and we lose that wonder and the delight of everyday things. We used to see winter as a playground but for many as they get older they only see the snow and feel the cold. So they pack their bags and head south.

There are of course times when winter seems endless but in our hearts we know spring will come. Then once again the world around us will have that touch of magic. There always arrives for us that special day, that special moment, when you note that there is a greenness to all the countryside. Your heart will be filled with a fullness that is hard to describe. Your spirit rises; and once again you know it is good to be alive. Perhaps all this means that you too, like the world around you, are opening up just like spring. You smile more and you are more cheerful. The winter gloom has gone.

No matter how long or cold the winter, spring is sure to follow.

Linda

and

My Tulips

Linda and My Tulips

The Driving Shed and Henhouse

Away back in the mid nineteen fifties, we decided we needed to put a fence across the yard between the house and the barn buildings. There was a smaller barn-like building sitting on the ground straight in from the laneway. We called it a driving shed. Attached to the south side of the driving shed was the henhouse and therein lay the problem. It housed a couple hundred free-ranging old biddies that had the idea they owned the place. They thought there was no better place to scratch for bugs and worms than in my flowerbeds. As you know that is a no no.

There is nothing like coming in at noon for dinner and finding ten feet of your petunia bed shredded to ribbons. It was war, me or them. I chased them off towards the henhouse with the broom, showing no mercy as I whacked them on their rears.

However there was one old biddy that was especially persistent and I am sure she was the leader of the flock. She was blind in one eye so I guess she thought she had my sympathy, as I would pick her up and gently carry her off. Unlike the rest of the birds she would not shoo when you told her to shoo. She was stubborn and would just sit down and wait for you to remove her. It just seems unmanly to whack anything when it sits or lies down.

At that time there was also heavy traffic in the yard. You see I had 3 sisters and every weekend when the boyfriends arrived the yard looked like a used car lot. Whenever I wanted out there would be a car parked behind me. Thus the time had come to fence the hens out and define a parking lot more boyfriend friendly.

It was early fall when we drew up a plan as to where we would place the fence. We also decided on two wood-picket gates that closed onto each other in the centre of the yard directly in front of the lane so it would look just right. A special woven fence that chickens could not get through would go from the north end of the barnyard to the picket gate, and then again from the other side of the gate into what was then a part of the orchard. From there the fence was to go back towards the house. This would solve the problem of encroaching hens and also enlarge the area for parking for the ever-present boyfriends.

It also gave me a whole new area to landscape for flowerbeds. Oh happy me.

Dad and I picked some nice uniform-size cedar posts and spaced them out every so far apart across the yard. Then we went to the bush and cut some ash poles and put them between the tops of the posts all the way around the yard. Then the fence went on. We also placed a small picket gate to the south of the two big gates so we could go to and fro to the barn with ease. All the while the busy old hens looked on with curiosity and interest.

It was taking shape and looked very neat when it was done.

Then came the landscaping. I brought up trailer load after trailer load of rich black earth from the bush and put a flowerbed all along the inside of the fence from one side of the yard to the other. The old hens looked on bug-eyed with great anticipation.

I found an old steel tractor wheel rim about five feet across and a foot high and put it in the south corner. In the centre of that I dug a hole and put up a flag pole about 20 feet high. When that was done I planted some grass seed in the new area.

Then I painted the gates, the post and the pole at the top of the fence white. It showed off great even from the road. I have always liked yard work and I was very proud of my work.

That fall I spent some of my hard cash on 300 tulip bulbs in six different shades. I planted the tulips with great care arranging the colours so that when they came in bloom there would be a design.

Winter came on and that area of the yard always received a good coat of snow. Thus my bulbs were kept from freezing over the winter. The next spring they were peeking out of the ground early like peas down a row. I could hardly wait for them to bloom. All spring from day to day I was able to follow their growth as I went to and fro from the barn doing chores.

Once again as it was spring the hens were out free roaming the far side of the fence and for a time my flowerbeds seemed very safe. After a few weeks though the old blind hen who by now had earned the name of "Pecky," discovered if she walked all the way down the fence to the north end of the barnyard she could get through the wider woven fence. Then she made her way all the way back on this side of the fence to get to the house. She would even end up at the kitchen door looking for us. Time and time again I would pick her up and toss her back over the fence. She would crash down and then ruffle her feathers and turn around in a circle clucking angrily at me. Yet every time I was working on her side of the fence she would turn up at my feet. In time we all learned to love her.

While all the other hens were sold off every fall and replaced with pullets we saved old Pecky's life for many years. She lived well into old age and was sold along with the farm in 1961 to Aaron Penner.

About now I should introduce you to my niece Linda.

Linda was a sweet child and the first child in our family. We waited for her to be born and from that day on we have loved her dearly. As a little girl she loved to visit the farm and grandpa and grandma, and I would say they doted on her. She could do no wrong and I must admit that even Uncle Jack thought so too, well until one day. I will have to tell you about that.

The tulips were all in bloom all across the yard. They were by now a showcase for all my hard work. Everyone who dropped in would walk over to the bed and ooh and aah and I of course stood by very proud to show my tulips off.

It was in the spring of about 1946 when my mom had to go into the hospital in St Marys for an operation. One of those operations I can't tell you about here.

Of course Linda could see our concern so she was worried about her grandma.

Dad and I had work to do at the barn and so we left Linda alone at the house.

Some time later I went back to the house to check on her and there she was sitting on the lawn beside a massive pile of tulips. I could not believe it. She had got the scissors and cut off the tops of all the tulips. They were left with about two inches of stems. I was so angry I could not contain myself. I made a beeline for her and thankfully dad came through the gate just in time to stop me to save Linda.

Linda narrowly escaped the tanning of her lifetime, and me a lifetime of shame.

By now she understood what she had done and was crying. She said she had cut them to take to grandma at the hospital, thinking they would help make her better.
She was only about 5 years old, but she remembers those tulips to this day. She also remembers Uncle Jack was very unhappy with her that day.

Of course tulips bloom but once a year and after they bloom you have to leave the leaves and stems standing until they start to dry because while doing so it is forming next year's bulbs. So everyday while going to and fro from the barn or field I was able to walk by my topless tulips and think of my dear little niece

Linda has grown up and has found out she too, has a green thumb. Thus she surrounds her lot with many flowerbeds.

In the spring if I go to visit her, she tells me to stay away from her tulips beds.

The Tulip Extravaganza

The Tulip Extravaganza

By my niece - Linda (Graver) Canniff

I was the first niece to tug on my Uncle Jack's heartstrings, to surprise him and at times even shock him. He was always happy to see me when I came to visit. He wore a huge grin on his face and gave me a big bear hug coming and going. He was and still is one of my favorite people in this world.

One bright sunny day my family left me to visit at grandpa and grandma's farm on the old Mitchell road near Motherwell where my Uncle Jack also lived.

I loved to run outside to play on the farm. There was so much space and beauty. I felt loved and safe but at the same time "free" as a bird. I was very young and I didn't know all the names for all of Uncle Jack's and my grandma's flowers. I do remember I did know the snowball bush and the roses. They were so gorgeous just like my grandma who tended them.

The sad part was at this time my grandma was in the hospital in St Marys sick. She was to have an operation and because I was just a little girl I couldn't see her. I gazed at the many wonderful coloured tulips going all the way across the yard and I thought how great grandma would feel if I sent them to her. Surely it would help her to get better sooner. My grandma loved flowers so I was sure this was a great idea. I hastily plucked the tulips heads off from every stem I could find, leaving behind beds of nice leafy bald tulips. I gathered the flowers in my skirt and placed them in a pile on the lawn.

About now Uncle Jack came racing from the barn yelling.

"No! No! No! Oh no! All my tulips are gone, you have ruined them".

To say the least, he gave me heck, but the worst was I had never, never seen Uncle Jack angry before, much less with me. I was a bit afraid and very tearful.

Right then my grandpa came from the barn through the yard gate to see what was going on. Uncle Jack pointed out to grandpa that I had taken all the tulip heads off and there were none left to see. He pointed his finger at me and said it was my fault and I was never, ever to touch his flowers again.

When I could find my voice I squeaked out that I had picked the tulips to take to grandma in the hospital so she would get better faster.

I must have looked pitiful and I was very sad to be in such trouble with my Uncle Jack. It was really out of character for him to be like this.

Grandpa was truly touched by my plight. He gave me a smile and told me that it was nice that I thought of grandma and wanted to cheer her up while she was sick.
He understood and I felt such relief. He gave me a hug and told me that the tulips would grow back next year. Grandpa told me he would see that grandma got some of the flowers. I am sure if he showed her them all she would have passed away.

I learned 3 things that day
1. Uncle Jack loves his flowers and you must never, never touch them or he could get very mad.
2. If you truly in your heart know you are doing something good for someone you love, it will all work out in the end.
3. No matter what cards Uncle Jack held, my Grandpa Cooke trumped Uncle Jack every time.

A few years later my dear grandma was in the hospital again due to her out of control diabetes. I was staying a few days with grandpa and Uncle Jack. This was on the second farm on the Mitchell Road just south of the village of Fullarton.

Note from Jack - (*This was before her Uncle Jack went to Barber College in 1963 So as Linda was born in 1951 she would only be about 11*)

I wanted to be grown up and help grandpa and Uncle Jack out doing whatever I could. I helped with the meals and doing dishes. I remember I helped wash eggs.

One of those days I found a piecrust already made and a lemon pie filling so I made it up for supper. My grandpa and Uncle Jack were all smiles and thanked me as they sat down for supper. When it came time for dessert Uncle Jack took a bite of the pie and grimaced as if in pain. He was making a comment that there was something badly wrong with the pie. Grandpa was eating his pie and he said to Uncle Jack, "Never mind, ---- Linda made this pie for us --- so it is good ---eat it up." Poor Uncle Jack he shoved it in and sucked it up!

I did feel sorry for him this time because it really did taste "terrible." The piecrust apparently was ancient and grandma had meant to throw it out. By now it was just not meant for human consumption.

These guys were on their own and never thought of checking the cupboards and fridge before turning a kid like me loose in the kitchen. I am sorry I didn't just throw it out. To this day I chuckle to myself as I recall the look on Uncle Jack's face while he was trying to choke down that pie. All because he did not want to hurt my feelings. You would think he would have been a faster learner. Once again grandpa trumped my Uncle Jack.

I do remember there was a time in particular that I deserved a whipping, but of course I didn't get it. Ah such was life on the farm and I have so many great memories of both those farms where my grandparents lived in succession.

One day Uncle Jack and I were walking hand in hand going back the rocky laneway to fetch the cows in the fields beyond the farm buildings. He told me not to get too close to the single strand of barbed wire strung along the side of the lane and above all warned me not to touch it.

Of course I just had to touch it and a strange jolt went through my arm and Uncle Jack's feet left the ground as he did a jig. I thought it was hilarious and funny. He yelped like a new puppy. I was told not to do that again. Now I knew what happens when you touch an electric fence and I thought Uncle Jack was making a big deal out of it. So off we went hand in hand down the lane and I was very happy. It was one of those beautiful sunny days you can get lost in. All about us the butterflies and bird flittering about and I was happy to be with my Uncle Jack and totally distracted in the world about me.

So I couldn't help myself, I touched it again! The jolt went through my arm and visited Uncle Jack once more. He did his yelp and danced a jig again.
I laughed I just could not contain myself.

Oh it can be truly painful and humbling to be a good uncle.

He warned me then that we would turn back and he would take me home if I didn't behave. So I behaved as we finished the business of getting the cows and going back to the barn. I remember how the cows would follow a leader one behind the other all the way back to the barn. They were so huge, so why wouldn't they just run off to anywhere they wanted to go. Well the truth is that the cows behaved better than I did that day.

These are childhood "forever" memories that I shared with my Uncle Jack. They are what relationships are built on. He makes me feel special, even though I share him now with several other nieces and nephews and their families. I am the oldest so I can remember further back. I used to sit on the piano bench along side Uncle Jack listen to him sing and play along on the piano in awe.

Uncle Jack traveled a lot in his youth and made many friends for life. He was first a farmer then a carpenter, a painter, a cowboy, a traveler and an apartment custodian and a finally a barber and now in retirement he adds to all this a writer.

Uncle Jack lives in London and has beautiful flower boxes on his condo balcony every season – so remember, look but don't touch.

Jack Cooke is many, more things then I can describe here, but to me he will always be that lovable "Uncle Jack" that I love. He has earned his stripes.

I tell you now, "He can't be trumped."

Our Ever

Changing World

Our Ever Changing World

When my sisters and I were growing up on the farm a visit to the big city was the highlight of the year. Somehow we managed to spend a weekend each year at my dad's sisters place my Aunt Maude and Uncle Guy's 20243 Alcoy St. Detroit.

I hold this vision of a morning many years ago while visiting my Aunt Maude's.

The war was over and Detroit was a thriving, booming vibrant city. You could feel it and you could see it all around you. The American dream was quite alive and it was right there encompassing me everywhere I looked. It was a very humbling experience for a kid off a sleepy farm in the heart of rural Old Ontario.

In the early morning the sun was rising over the healthy graceful elm trees that lined the streets on both sides of Alcoy in this relatively new sub-division.
Mid-way down the block there was a milk wagon being pulled by a handsome black Percheron horse. The milkman sharply dressed, was going from house to house with his wire basket full of glass milk bottles. There was a happy energy in the spring of his step as he marched with vigor down the street.

Each house had a little door built into the wall near the side door. This little door opened out onto the driveway. Inside on a shelf would be yesterday's empty milk bottles. Inside one bottle would be the money for today's milk. No one worried that someone might raid the bottles and take the money, it just didn't happen. I can't explain it to you any better than to say, it was simply the way we were. There was a certain divine honour for the need to respect one another's needs; it was simply the mode of the day. Without it you were a nobody.

There is something picture perfect about this scene; a fresh sunny morning, and a milkman in a crisp uniform going door to door on a tree-lined street while the well-behaved horse followed him up pulling the milk wagon. Life was indeed sweet.

Later the mailman, also dressed in his crisp blue uniform would walk from door to door under the watchful, waiting eyes of everyone up or down the street. He was known by name and respected by all as a part of the working community.

Perhaps it was something left over from the war, but there was a certain amount of order in our lives and the community and everyone was expected to live by it.

It seemed in those year while I was growing up everyone who worked in a trade proudly wore a uniform. A uniform as a rule was white or blue or a combination of white and blue. Most tradesmen at that time wore an officer-peeked cap. The milkman, the

fireman, the policeman and the mailman all wore a similar suit with a medium blue shirt and a dark tie and oh yes, the cap. Likewise everyone else from the Salvation Army, the elevator man to the janitor wore navy blue suits. I believe the idea was a uniform not only identified them but also helped them to believe in themselves and command a certain amount of attention and respect.
Even our local miller wore a striped miller's cap and huge striped bib overalls all summer and coveralls all winter. He looked every bit his part, a miller.

Not to be outdone, the barbers wore a crisp white jacket with a crossover front, with buttons on the side ending on the top of the shoulder. I remember how great the local barbers looked in their uniform. It helped to inspire me to one day be a barber. The druggist too, in every drug store also wore a similar jacket.

Waitresses wore a little cap-like thing on their head and a tiny apron.

I remember getting gas at a local gas station at Russeldale by Highway 23 and the owner of the station always dressed in a company uniform. Likewise my friend Ross Parrot who owned a Supertest Station on Main Street in Mitchell wore a Supertest uniform with pride. Everyone who was anyone seemed to dress for the part. Have you not heard it said, "He was dressed like a banker, or dressed like a funeral parlour director"? It seemed dress was recognized as a vital part of the trade. That is you can't cut hair dressed like a used car salesman or a butcher. It was thought if you dressed for the part, as it would help draw business to you.

Then for a number of years everything fell apart. "I wonder what happened."

It seems we came out of the depression of the thirties with not much more than a shirt on our back. Then in 1939 we were pushed into a world war. Many young men for the first time in their lives wore a suit and they wore it proudly. I was just old enough to see the pride they took in wearing their Canadian uniform, be it the Army the Air Force or the Navy. My dad and mom were given a number of pictures of nephews in uniform and they were displayed on the piano top for many years.

They say dress does not make a man, - Perhaps not always, but add to a uniform a job that puts a few dollars in his pocket and it will bring out the best in him.

The boys came home from war to find the country's economy booming and jobs were available. It was not hard to get a man who was used to wearing a military uniform into another uniform when it offered a job and a paycheck. Then again because he was used to shining everything from buttons to shoes in the military it was easy to get him to take care of his everyday uniform and to take pride in it.

For a number of years after the Second World War there was peace and prosperity. The veterans came home from the war ready to get married and to raise a family. In the late 1940's there was a baby boom of almost 4 children in every family. The government introduced the baby bonus of $5.00 a month for every child under 6. This would be equal to about $60.00 a month today. Children under 9 yrs. received $6.00. Under 12 it was $7.00 and children from 13 to 15 were paid $8.00. The baby bonus only paid full payment for 4 children. The 5th child affected the payout to all the rest.

There were new homes and new cars and it seemed as if the good lord had granted us a new life. It was the kind of life our grandparents never had and never dared to dream of. The young parents greeted the winds of change with open trust. They were sure the future was solid and would only get better. Thus they moved rapidly forward into the 1960's.

I graduated in the fall of 1963 from Droulards Barber College in Windsor and took over a small barbershop on Wellington Road in south London. For my first haircuts I got $1.00 for children and $1.25 for adults.

Every morning when I arrived at work I proudly donned my crisp white barber jacket. I remember those early years of the sixties as happy years…. a time when everything was going well for me, but trouble was brewing down the road. In the mid to late sixties the teenagers first started to wear their hair longer and longer and then started to reject haircuts all together. They began to think the longer the hair the better they looked and that they would never need to get a haircut again. Many of the very best barbers I knew had to close shop and find another job.

For a time it seemed like a cruel joke that I had spent my time and money to become a barber. No one seemed to understand or care that you were not making a living. You never heard of a barber going to the government hat in hand saying,
"Help Me."

Mothers brought their little boys in for haircuts and they wanted the hair cut with a cute little calf lick up-front just like daddy's used to be. The kids of course didn't want this at all and also they were aware their older brothers hated haircuts so they decided they did too. Thus they gave the barber a tough time while in the chair.

Business went from bad to worse, as the hair got longer. Added to all this teenagers started to wear outlandish bright pattern shirts and vests and tight jeans. Just when you thought it couldn't get worse they added platform shoes.

It was really a sight to see guys over six feet tall in bright dazzling shirts and tight jeans wearing platform shoes. Within a few years it seemed our common sense, square, stable world had gone mad. Welcome to the 60's.

The younger mailmen got caught up in all this too. They didn't want to wear a crisp uniform and they didn't want to get a haircut. Before long you couldn't tell a mailman with his bag of letters from a hippie with his bag of pot and whatever. Young people started carrying shoulder bags at that time and years later it led to the backpacks we see young people carrying today. It leads me to wonder how did our grandfathers manage to get along all day with nothing more then a change purse in the hip pocket and a pocket watch.

When the schools insisted on rules for haircuts and a dress code many of the teens took off for parts unknown.

The streets of downtown were full of long-haired kids and teens who didn't want to go to school and young men and women who really didn't want to work. Every night all summer hundreds of long-haired kids slept in the streets in London. They called themselves hippies. It wasn't just the local kids and young folks; they came to the city from all over the country small towns and villages and some even from out of province. On Monday mornings the mailman, who once looked honest and honorable and proud of his job now looked like a hippie the morning after.

Years later people have tried to analyze just what happened. They say hindsight is always one of the greater things we gain, as we get older but it is of little comfort. Many feel that after the war there was a generation of children born into a time of great prosperity. Perhaps it was the first of its kind for Canadians.

Parents and grandparents who never had much as a child for themselves could now afford to buy thing for themselves and for their children and grandchildren too.

It seemed the young folks of the day were set on breaking all those golden rules and traditions their parents and grandparents held so dear. They dressed weird.
They smoked pot and took pills they called speed. It became a culture and they swore there was no harm in it. They stayed out late or all night or just left home. They had found a great new freedom and many of the young people were not able to handle it. They went on long weekend binges of drugs and booze and were in no shape to turn up on Monday mornings for work or school or even to go home. This of course was a great worry for moms and dads, whose only thoughts were,

"Where is my son or daughter tonight?"

Indeed, there was a great need to worry as they watched their kids self-destruct.

It destroyed many of those young people and they are among the homeless on our streets today crying out for help, as they don't feel they have their fair share of Canada's wealth. However back in the late 1960's and 70's they knew it all and you could not tell them anything. They were totally into a mindless good-time- dream world that had no future. It was a fact; they had no fear and gave no thought to the future. Today was all that mattered. They were anti-society, and anti-social to the adult world and to law and order. They damaged their minds and in the end stripped themselves of hope and pride. Now they bear the fruit of the life they wasted.

Getting old has its blessings as you learn not to despair. You come to know that "This too will pass away".

We have just passed through a time when youth thought looking disgusting was the way to go. Tattoos and ear and nose and nipple rings were" the in thing" along with pants worn with the crotch down almost to the knees, while the moon shone.. It was hard to believe how it all came about. But like the 60's it did, and like the 60's ----

"It too passed away".

In praise of the day is that today's young people are looking good and going to school or working at jobs. They have a new pride in the way they look.

Once again uniforms are being worn with pride, be it the armed forces the police, the firemen or Tim Hortons.

Yes, it seems even haircuts are back in style.

The Field Of Dreams and The Shadows Of War

The Field Of Dreams and The Shadows Of War

The Field Of Winter Wheat

It was the spring of 1941, the war was going badly in Europe and my grandfather had just passed away after a long illness of cancer. After my grandfather's death my dad took over the family farm, mortgage and all. I don't have any remembrance of him feeling very happy about it. Up until then he had rented the farm from his dad. The way things had been I guess he knew if all else failed he could always ask for more time to pay the rent or he could just walk away.

In all truth if he had really wanted to farm he should have been happy, because I think he got the chance he needed without a lot of red tape. Instead I had the feeling that he looked at it as a trap. Now there was no way out for him. He had to farm and Mr. Bothwell would be waiting every fall for his mortgage payment.

Dad had rented the farm throughout the thirties, through the years of the great depression, and it had taken its toll on him as it did on many other farmers. I well remember listening to dad and mom talking to the neighbours who had similar problems of just keeping afloat. They worked hard all year and yet they were forever just managing to hang on, one year at a time. All the time they hoped and prayed for better times, that the crop next year would be bigger and the price for every thing just a wee bit better. They gave hope to each other in times of great need and if "truth" be told they needed each other's confidence in their seemingly never ending battle to be tough and hang in there. On top of that my dad had not entirely managed to win his battle against polio which he had in the early nineteen thirties. It took him many years to recover.

When August of 1941 came dad decided to plow down the pasture field at the rear of the old farm. He worked it down well and made a good seedbed, ready for fall wheat. The field was about 17 1/2 acres. Most farmers planted a few acres of winter wheat, as a rule about ten acres. Mom had to have some wheat for her hens as she always fed them about one quarter wheat and the rest oats and barley. The good thing was that since 1939 after several years of heat and drought the weather was more favourable for crops. Also because of the war the prices of all farm products were getting better. So with the hope of a good crop of wheat and a fair price this field of wheat would help with the mortgage payment next fall.

The winter wheat most people were growing at that time was called Durham.

I would be 12 years old going on 13 in October of 1941. When you're a kid you don't look at your parents' heavy discussions as dreams of the future. You're more inclined to feel they are overly concerned about their problems of the present.
However I guess I was beginning to pay attention to what was being said and at times I found myself trying to put it all together. I was concerned so it bothered me.
I remember my mom trying to convince me that everything was going to be alright or ok, and next year was going to be better, just you wait and see.

I should not have said OK as you see OK had not been invented just yet. It was one of those things that came to us from the service men in training to fight the war. I well remember my sister Laurine coming home from her first year in high school and when she was asked about something she said, "It was OK".
After hearing it a number of times my dad and mom were concerned about this new word and wondered just what she was learning in high school. She assured them it was not a bad word. If fact it was ...well ….OK. That was the very first time I ever heard the word OK and it was by my sister Laurine.

Just as my mom had told me, outside of our everyday worry about the war, (World War Two) things just continued to get a bit better each year down on the farm. There were some things we accepted, as we could not do anything about it.

These were such things as food ration, which was a part of the war effort so we accepted it quite willingly. People did the best they could and I don't feel they complained a great deal. You see the Liberal government under Prime Minister Mackenzie King issued us little books of stamps to be used for certain items that had to be rationed in order to feed England and our troops overseas.

It was in 1942 that they first rationed gasoline and butter. Then followed the rationing of sugar, coffee and meat. Often you were able to switch coupons with your neighbour. Let us say if he did not drink coffee and you didn't use much sugar you exchanged coupons. Some older people didn't drive their cars very much so they gave their gas coupons to their friends. I'm not sure how it all worked out, but that is how we won the war. I guess you might call it, hard work and co-operation.

It was important to the war effort that farmers were able to buy all the gas they needed to put in their crops and take them off. So the government had the farm gas coloured purple and left the car gas white. Pity the poor guy who got caught with purple gas in his car. They didn't take kindly to cheating. Of course there were always a few who had to try. Perhaps a couple gallons of purple gas added to a tank of white gas might go undetected if it got checked.

I remember once when we had to drive to Hamilton to my Uncle Jack Butson's for the Butson family reunion when dad filled the gas tank with fuel oil and then added some mothballs. Someone told him it helped to keep the smell down. The trick in burning fuel oil in the car was to start the car on gasoline and then fill the tank with the fuel oil. You see a car or tractor won't start on fuel oil but will run ok once its started, - Just don't stop your motor, as then the car would not start again. Dad drove to Hamilton and then filled the tank with gas while the motor was still running. This worked fine, but the car gave off a lot of foul smelling exhaust fumes all the way down to Hamilton. To make matters worse both my dad and grandpa Butson smoked a pipe and I had to sit in the front seat between them. I was sure I was going to die of suffocation. When I complained they thought it was funny.

The field of wheat was sowed in early September, and within a few days it was a sea of green. Later in the fall it looked like a promise of a great crop for the next year. A number of deer came out of the bush every evening to browse on it. At first we were a bit worried they might harm it, but upon inspection dad noted no damage. Snow came down and covered it all winter protecting it from deep frost and cold winds. The deer continued to paw the snow and browse on the wheat each evening. We let them be. We realized that they had to have a way to survive.

Spring came and our field of wheat had survived the winter well and looked marvelous from the end of the lane all the way to the bush. Soon it was time to sow the rest of the crop. Most farmers in those days grew what they called mixed grain…. that is the oats and barley together. Then since there were still horses on the farm it was only right to sow a few acres of pure oats. Working horses loved their oats and expected them at the end of the day. (Thus the old saying) "Be sure you're worth your oats."

Dad grew a variety of great early oat called Alaska, and sometimes he grew Carter. For many years OAC barley was considered the very best barley to grow then Montcalm became very popular for malting barley.

Some farmers would apply to Labatts and get a contract to grow malting barley. At the time I pondered this as the same people dropped their temperance envelope into the collection plate on Sundays at the United Church in support of temperance and abstinence. The first year my dad grew a field of contract malt barley I remember asking him to explain this to me. I was told in so many words that small boys ask too many questions about things that do not concern them. In time I too learned that hard times sometimes brought on the need to survive - any which way.

About now all Canadians were very concerned about the war as Germany was walking out in all directions in Europe. They seemed unstoppable. In the meanwhile troops from all over the world from what was then called The British Empire were gathering and huddled down in England in training for the invasion. In June of 1941 the Germans had attacked Russia and by mid 1942 they were deep within Russia. The Russians fought bravely but were ill equipped to fight the war against the well-equipped Germans. In 1941 Ford Motors stopped building new cars and started to build bombers for the war. New car production never started again until after the war in 1946. By the end of the war there were many old cars on the road. Cars that were just hanging together, rusted out with holes you could shove your fist through. No one seemed to care as we were all in this war together.

This was the first year that my grandfather was not there to help my dad. Actually dad and my grandfather had never worked very well together but rather co-existed to get the job done as so many fathers and sons do who are forced to work close together. As yet dad was not fully recovered from his bout of polio in the early thirties, so no doubt he missed his father now that he was gone. I was still too young to be of great help as I was in my last year of public school.

On a farm about 2 miles north of our farm on the Mitchell Road just where the road turned sharply to the west because of the bend in the Thames river, there lived a lone bachelor by the name of Alonzo Hart. Alonzo it seemed had no interest in working his farm as he would rather work off the farm as a hired man. He and dad knew each other and for a number of years while I was in my early teens Alonzo was dad's hired man. This worked out well for dad and Alonzo too.

Spring turned to summer and our great field of wheat was fast maturing. Its large heads started to turn colour long before the end of June and by my mom's birthday July the 10th it was ready to cut with the binder. By now my dad had made a short tongue for the old International binder so he could pull it with the 10/ 20 McCormick Dearing tractor. My grandfather had coached my mom for several years on how to operate the grain binder and he was proud to tell people Reta could tie a better sheaf of grain then anyone else in the country.

To ride the binder my mom would don an old pair of dad's overalls and a shirt, then a straw hat. It was strange to see my mom dressed this way for you see at that time no women wore slacks or long pants. It was considered very un-ladylike.

Over the years it seemed it was often on my mom's birthday July the 10th that the wheat had to be cut and I felt sad that she had to ride the binder on her birthday. Many years later when she was in her 80's I mentioned this to her she laughed and said." No Jack you got it all wrong, you see I was happy the day we cut the wheat, - because after all it was the wheat I was going to feed to my hens for the next year."
So dad drove the tractor and mom rode the binder and Alonzo and I stooked.
I was always a very strong boy so this worked out well and by the end of the day we had the field of wheat cut and a large part of it stooked.

When you cut wheat with the binder you cut it just before it is too ripe so that your packers on the binder do not shake out the wheat. The wheat in the sheaf then sits in the stook for its final maturing stage and hardens. In other words nature is allowed to finish its work. Nowadays when they combine the grain they wait until the grain is very ripe and dry enough to put in the storage bin right away.

Dad had a huge old railway red wooden threshing machine. I have never been sure of the make, but I remember the faded words printed on the side "Gibson".
It weighed tons and had to be planked on the barn floor so as not to break through. It always scared me to death whenever it had to be moved.

As dad needed the wheat straw for cattle bedding we would barn thresh and blow the straw out into the barnyard in front of the barn. Building a great stack in front of the barn was considered the work of art. People visiting would admire it.
Dad took great pride in building a stack. When I think of it now I know it was not easy for him to do it as he had one very bad leg from his bout with polio.

We still used our team of horses "Queen and old Frank" on the tall wooded spoke wheel wagon. At that time we just could not see that anything could work better and certainly not cheaper than a good team of horses and a wagon. These old wagons were hard to pull as when loaded the wheels cut deep into the soft earth. They didn't ride over the top of the soil as rubber tires do. A good team will follow the row of grain stooks up and down the field all by themselves. All you had to do was say, "Giddy-up" and "Whoa."

The sheaves of wheat one by one had to be pitched onto the wagon and a load built with great care. We easterners for some reason always built our wagonloads of grain with pride, straight up on both sides and topped it off to perfection.

Many years later when I was working out west, I discovered how to build my own load on what they called a basket rack. They laughed at the way we did it in the east for as they said the object of the game was to get the grain to the machine. They then added with great delight, "It isn't a beauty contest."

Many wagonloads of wheat sheaves were drawn from the back field of the farm to the bank barn. Too large a load made it very hard for the horses to dash up the gangway and on into the barn. Poor old Frank was getting old and I'm sure he dreaded each time he had to be urged into a trot to climb that steep gangway into the barn.

Alonzo and dad worked in the field and brought the wagon loaded with wheat to the barn. Upon arriving at the barn dad got off the load to start the tractor and soon the old threshing machine would be roaring away and shaking on the barn floor. The belts would be flying and the dust rising. The horses would be standing within inches of the roaring machine. This is why I love horses, they can be taught to trust. Amid all that vibration, noise, dust and dirt they stood there in quiet trust.

Never in my lifetime, would I break trust with a horse, it seems a sacred thing.

Alonzo fed the sheaves to the machine while my dad looked after it and then every so often he would climb up onto the straw stack to build it. As for me I was on hand in the granary each time the load of grain appeared. I kept the grain away from the pipe and filled the bins.

Our days were filled with hard but satisfying work. My mom put a special effort into seeing our meals were super great during harvest time. After the day's work was finished and our supper over, there were always cows to milk and pigs to feed. The hired man was expected to help with that too as although he was working for a day's wages he was also getting his meals and an overnight bed. At times when it looked like rain my mom and my sisters would start the milking early and we men-folk worked late. That's when it was great to have 3 sisters.

For a while in the evening we would listen to the many great radio programs which all we oldies remember clearly to this day. Some of our favourites were the half hour program such as Fibber McGee and Molly sponsored by Johnson's Wax, or the Amos and Andy show that few of us realized was a black African American show. Campbell's Soup and Rinso Soap sponsored it

Before we went off to bed we would always check on the news, especially for news on the war. We knew the invasion of Europe was going to happen and very soon. It was not going well for the Russians. The Germans drove the Russians back and were almost to Moscow. Tens of thousand of Russians had taken a stand.

Moscow would not be invaded. The Russians, men and women young and old were ill-equipped for war and were slaughtered by the thousands. Regardless they rallied to their slogan, "We have Moscow behind us, we have no right to retreat."

In those days it just seemed there was no easy way to do anything. Now that we had our winter wheat safely in the granary we had to bag it in burlap bags and then load in onto a truck to haul to the grain elevator. Almost all of our collection of burlap sacks had been used for what we called chop, ground grain. It seems I have always been allergic to dusty things and one was the dust from ground grain. I just hated to be near the grain grinder or chop bags. Yet there I was holding the chop bags while my dad filled them with wheat with a large pail. A bag of wheat is heavy and at 14 coming 15 that fall I could scarcely handle it. It had been a good crop and we had about a thousand bushels of beautiful wheat. We left what we felt my mom needed for her hens and bagged the rest. The aisle of the granary was soon piled high with bags and bags of wheat.

When it was all bagged, it was time to called John G Scott our faithful ole trucker in the village of Russeldale. In a day or two he arrived with his rather ancient old green truck on which the rack was held together with wire.

He would slowly back up to the granary door high on the south side of our barn. Now John G always had his own way of doing things. While some people at times would complain it didn't seem to change anything. He would always back up until he smacked into the stone wall of your barn with a hard whack. When you hit a stone wall you stop rather abruptly but at least you would know you had arrived, and of course that was the point. This had always worked well for John G. all of his trucking years. However our old barn wall and those of many other barns in the area were taking a beating and some were starting to crumble.

It was now the real work of loading was about to begin. We put a wide granary board down from the granary door onto the truck floor and then slid the bags down. I am not sure how many loads of this bagged wheat left the granary but I think dad sold perhaps 800 bushels of wheat that fall. When he took the last load in I rode in with John G and his truck and dad followed with his car. My dad drove in with his black 1938 Ford with loose fenders and many holes. Even so we knew as many others did it would have to do until after the war.

The wheat was taken to Ferg Levies Mill, far to the south end of Mitchell. At that time there was no bridge over the Thames on the south end of town so we had to drive into town and over the bridge then down the main street and turn south at the post office.

To me it seemed the mill had been there forever and I knew Ferg well to see him. His brother owned a well known grocery store up town. Both men looked very much alike except Ferg always had on his dusty millers coveralls two sizes too big while his brother wore a large white apron in his grocery store.

Ferg was a short-legged man with a wide girth at the middle. His striped miller's cap was always perched on top of his head. There were two great sized pockets on the front of his pants and the one on the right always stuck out noticeably. Everyone local was aware that Ferg had a fat roll of bills stuck in that pocket. It was often said that the roll was large enough to choke a horse and seeing was believing. He always paid cash for everything. It was a sight to see him peel off the bills one after the other from that roll and hand it to my dad, and yet not make a dent in it.

Certainly it was a sight for a poor farm boy to see. I remember thinking at that time, - "Some day something bad is going to happen to you because of that wad of bills." Years later I understand he did get hit on the head and robbed.

Because of the war and the need to feed the ever-increasing army in England the price of wheat was the best it had been in years. In the thirties we had sold winter wheat for 45 cents a bushel. I am not sure just what dad got that fall for his wheat but I'm sure well over a dollar, possibly more than $1.25 a bushel as he took home about $1,000.00 right off Ferg's fat roll of bills.

As it was a Saturday the banks closed early so my dad had this thousand dollars in his possession until Monday morning.

That night we were to go to Ed and Joy Smith's and family for the evening. While the older folks player euchre in the kitchen we kids never seemed to have much trouble amusing ourselves with the run of the house.

After a time the conversation got around to dad's wheat and the thousand dollars. Dad told them he was afraid to leave it at home so he had hid it under the back seat of the car. I remember how fascinated they all were by so much money. Suddenly they all got up from the table and we kids followed them out to the car. Each one took the money in his or her hands to hold it just for a moment. Then before dad put it back under the car seat he handed it to me saying,

"Hold onto it for a minute, now you can always say you once had a thousand dollars in your hands."

I always felt at that time that field of wheat was more than dollars or bushels per acre. It was their dream and it had come true. I am not sure how much of that money ever got paid down on the mortgage but I do know life was getting better on the farm. I remember that year as the turning point from hardship to prosperity.

August was always a busy month on the farm and especially so in the 1940's as at that time most grains took more days to mature than the varieties we have today. So soon after the wheat was harvested the malted barley would start to ripen up followed by the mixed grain.

My dad had a silo and grew silage corn but very few if any local farmers in our area were yet growing corn as a cash crop or for cattle and hog feed. In fact corn combines had not been invented yet.

Things for us here in Canada were going on as usual and it seemed that good times were prevailing. For many of us it was unreal that across the ocean there was a war going on that in time might even come to us. At times we were almost lulled into believing nothing bad could possibly happen. Then on the evening of August the 19th 1942 we turned on the 6 o-clock news and found out that the allied armies had invaded the coast of Europe. Up until that time little was know about the whereabouts of the Canadian army and what was going on. The news was much slower in arriving than it is today but over time we found out that almost 5000 Canadians troops were stationed on the Isle of Wight and these Canadians on that day August 19,1942 invaded Dieppe. It was a disaster from the very start.

Most people at home thought that this was a real invasion, but we are told now it was actually done for two reasons. First it was to test the resistance of the local Germans army along the coast to an invasion, and second to make the Germans feel the need for more troops to defend that coast line and thus relieving the pressure on the Russians who were facing defeat deep within Russia.

Many people felt that the allies allowed the Germans and the Russians to fight on and on destroying each other, thus held off the invasion just because we were not sure that communist Russia was our friend either. At the same time they could not afford to let Germany take over Russia and then turn it against us. Such is war.

Of the almost 5000 Canadians that invaded Dieppe 907 were killed, 2210 managed to escape and returned to England and the rest, about 2500 were taken prisoners by the Germans. This defeat was a real blow to our army overseas and to Canadians here at home. Perhaps it was a wake-up call. Too long we had been lulled into feeling safe here in Canada afar off from Europe. We were well aware we were enjoying prosperity brought to us because of the war and up until now without paying the cost. In truth the war created good times for us financially.

The harvest was off and all things seemed to return back into a routine on the farm. Dad was back on the tractor working the seedbed for another year's field of wheat. I was back to school in September working hard in my last year of grade 8. My sister Laurine started high school that fall. There was no school bus yet so she had to board in town. She was very lucky as a cousin Mac and Jean Norris in Mitchell who lived not far from the high school offered to board her and spoiled her rotten.

That fall the government had the teachers sell us war stamps at 25 cents each. You were given a book and every week you were expected to buy a stamp or two and paste them in your book. When the book was full it was worth $5.00. That was a lot of money to a kid in 1942. Eventually you would be able to take the book to the bank and exchange it for cash plus whatever interest it had earned. For the older folks there were Victory Bonds, which were to be held for five years before cashing. The war was being fought on credit.

Soon the Red Cross got into the act and had school children knitting wool squares of a certain dimension and these were sewn together to make quilts for the army. Mothers were unraveling their old wool skirts and sweaters and anything woolen and sending balls of yarn to school with their kids to knit. The boys were expected to learn to knit too. There were some very crude looking parts to every quilt. I cannot imagine that these quilts were sent to our troops overseas. One might even hope they were sent to the enemy to inflict the pain of a dreadful itch or to weigh them down when the quilt got wet and drowned them. However I suppose the effort the kids put into it was good for them. They felt they had done something good to help win the war.

For us on the farm life went on and soon we would see the deer back on our field of wheat, and every now and then I would catch my dad and mom in quiet conversation.

I knew that once again they were looking to the future with dreams and somehow I just knew it had a lot to do with next year's field of wheat

Mixed Farming

As I

Remember It

Mixed Farming As I Remember It

Bill Stephens and His Team

There was a time when mixed farming was the norm everywhere in Ontario.

It was up and down the Mitchell Road and far and wide across the community. Each farmer had a combination of things he chose to work at. Every farmer had a dog a team of horses, milked a few cows, fed a few hogs and kept a few hens. They tended a garden and an orchard too. In everyway possible they were efficient.

It was indeed the farmer that invented the old saying,
"You never put all your eggs in one basket."

Old time farmers were a resourceful but fearful lot, as they did not want to take any chances on failure. By distributing their energy over a number of fields they felt they would always find a profit somewhere and thus they would survive. That in many ways was their real undoing as they worked themselves into an early grave trying to be, and to do, all things. Many farmers were as they say, 'A jack of all trades but a master of none'.

When spring came they tapped their maple trees to make maple syrup. All the while the cattle would still be in the barn and had to be tended to. Seeding time often arrived before the spiles were pulled and the sap buckets gathered from the trees. The lantern lights were shining in the barn in the early morning hours and again late at night. Once the season got underway the work was endless and they couldn't allow themselves to get behind or they might never get caught up all year.

The barnyard would be piled high with rich manure hauled from the stables over the winter. As soon as the fields were ready the horses were hitched to the manure spreader and soon there would be lots of great calluses built on the hands that laboured. For several weeks dad and my grandfather hauled, as they told us kids "sugar". When they came in for dinner they left their boots at the foot of the veranda steps but when they sat down for dinner oh how they smelled of ….sugar.

Everyone in the community would be aware of what they were doing as all morning the neighbors downwind were blessed with the true aroma of …. spring.

It was a glorious day when all the young cattle were turned out from the stables to their summer pasture and the cows were once again browsing in a meadow of sweet smelling alfalfa or red clover.

The henhouse door would be opened and the old biddies were free to roam once more. Life for all was good. Often the pigpen door was blocked ajar so the latest brood of little pigs could seek adventure and roam about the barnyard. They would follow each other in single file following a leader, venturing wherever their cute little button noses would lead them ……every day a bit farther and farther afield …. when suddenly something dire might accost them. Perhaps it would be the king of the barnyard, the old red rooster. He would not budge even for 12 nosy, cheeky little piglets. A painful peck on the nose of their brave inquisitive leader would send the whole brood squealing, flying frightfully back to the safety of the pigpen door. Little pigs though while disrespectfully cute, are just as rude, stubborn and inquisitive, so very soon they would be back outside heading off again on yet another adventure.

The colony house was made ready and perhaps a couple of hundred little day old chicks would arrive. They were little yellow fuzz balls that everyone loved to hold. This would be one of my mom's pet projects and I don't think she would have given it up to anyone. It was always her personal project and she tended it with loving care. Someday these lovable little creatures would put a constant flow of cash called "Egg Money" into her purse every week.

I can see my mom now; She would knock gently on the door to let them know she had arrived. You never moved swiftly amid a flock of wee chicks, and you must always be mindful of your feet. When they got to know you they thought of you as mother hen and they seemed to have no fear.

I used to think someone was in there with mom as you see mom would talk to the chicks. She shooed them, scolding them, blessed them and praised them. When she left the place there would be the sound of 200 little beaks pounding away at the feeders. It sounded much like distant pounding rain or the coming of a storm.

The fields of mixed grain along with the oats and barley would soon be a sea of green and about the 24th of May it was time to plant the silage corn. We planted ours with the grain drill, three rows at a time. A family of black birds and the odd old crow sat on the lane post eyeing the progress. Long before the field was finished they and all their country cousins would be strutting up and down the field in search of a row of corn seed. Once they found it they would walk right down the row taking out every kernel.

How did they know it was corn being planted in the field and how to find it? Well you see they had a grandpa too, and just like it was with my grandpa and me. Grandpa's tell you everything you must know to survive.

A few scarecrows might help to scare them away, but a shotgun worked even better.

Once the corn was a few inches high it had to be hoed and kept free of weeds. Weed spray you see had not been invented yet, but we did have an alternative, a hoe. Farmers spent many hours everyday under the hot sun hoe in hand hoeing corn.
After the corn was hoed a couple of times there was the hay to cut and haul to the barn. This would be in mid to late June the hottest time of the year. Then fall or winter wheat would be ready to be cut and stooked by the second week of July.

The cutting and stooking of the rest of the grain crop would soon follow. Of course the biggest happening of the whole year was soon to follow, the threshing.

It was the reason and the payback for all of our year's labour and investment. We looked forward to it with great expectation, but oh how relieved we were when it was over. If there was ever a time of respite from labour for the old time mixed farmer it might be right after his crop was safely off the fields and in his barn. Nevertheless I feel all too often this way of life of "Mixed Farming" was so deeply integrated within them that they felt guilty when they left the farm for a day or two as their conscience told them they were neglecting their duty. Work was a way of life.

Thank heavens for Sundays, as everyone got a chance to sleep in just a wee bit longer on Sunday mornings. After the morning chores were done, and after the pigpens were cleaned out, it was a day of rest. It was also the day you had to turn up at church with all the family and thank God for the just reward for your labour. Small wonder some of the best men I ever knew slept soundly through the whole church service. I'm sure God understood and blessed then deservingly with an hour of heavenly rest.

They worked at something all year round. It just seemed one thing always managed to overlap the other. The whole year was spent chasing from one thing to another like a dog chasing its tail. They only stopped on Sunday afternoons when they fell asleep in their pews or wherever or whenever they sat down   …. They were happy and they were content but they were also exhausted.

There were times when the weather held them up, but that only meant that the stables or calf pens got cleaned out. A good thing always seemed to get cancelled out by another.

Nothing was ever done the easy way as it just seemed muscles and manual labour were in style. It was backbreaking work with a wheelbarrow, hoe, fork or a shovel.
During a young farmer's active years very few took more then a one-day holiday.

I saw all this very early in my life. I watched my grandfather and grandmother get older and burdened down by what seemed like endless unrewarding labour. My dad and mom were following in their steps always hoping things would get better. I realize now that my dad and mom in their years had already seen good times and bad. So together as a young married couple they had faith in tomorrows.

Even at a tender age I was not sure I really wanted to farm and I thought that this alone was wicked of me. Loving my grandfather as I had and being the only boy I had this feeling within me that I was the heir and the caretaker of my grandpa's land. This farm was my home, the only home I had ever known. Yet I was insecure, I just could not see into a future.

For some reason my grandmother used to say,
"No rest for the wicked", and then hold her head up high and add, "and the righteous don't need any". I didn't quite understand this but I did know it came from the Bible and for some reason I always felt a lot more wicked then righteous.

My three sisters had already come to that conclusion. That is that I was wicked and I never argued with them. Yet I never doubted their love for me. I was irresistible.

In spite of all this I believe there is a time in childhood when you feel time stands still. A time when the days crawl by, a time when waiting for next weekend and Saturday night is like waiting on eternity. Life was indeed moving at a snail's pace……...

Our life is like the little snail…
Where we go we leave a trail.
The things we do and the things we say…
Are the trails we leave from day to day?

Author Unknown

Locked away in my mind was the knowledge that I was here ----forever.
I had always been young and I could not imagine myself
ever getting old.

Memories

Of

Christmas Past

Memories of Christmas Past

Sitting in my lazy-boy chair contemplating Christmas past, my thought drift back to the very first Christmases I can remember. As I was born in 1928 it would be those Christmases in the early nineteen thirties during the great depression that I remember. Money was scarce and my parents with 4 children could scarcely do more then feed and clothe us. Yet of all the Christmases I have ever known it is those Christmases I remember the most. I was not brought up with a cluster of toys about me and I had no expectations of many gifts under the tree. I suppose you might say as my true knowledge of Santa Claus increased so did the knowledge of my world about me. I knew, and I accepted it. We were poor. Having said that, it was no big deal.

Nearly all of our extended family and neighbours were in the same boat. We were dirt poor in dollars but oh what a wealth we had in our friendships.

There was a row of spruce trees stretching from the house to the Mitchell Road and every year we managed to get a beautiful Christmas tree from the top of one of them. To my sisters and me it was always the greatest tree in the world. Dad would place it in an old milk pail and pack it with bricks to hold it upright. Mom would bring out the few decorations she had saved from the Christmas before. I will always remember the two long ropes, one green and the other red. Then there was a box of beautiful delicate coloured balls, which smashed to bits if they fell to the floor. Foil icicles were saved from year to year and hung separately and hung long from the branches with care. From the tin foil of a package of Salada tea a five-point star was cut and placed atop the tree. As this was years before we had hydro, there were no string of lights on the tree, but you never miss what you never had. Our tree was beautiful.

Somewhere in the thirties we were each given a small celluloid animal to hang on the tree. One was a cow, one a goat, one a pig and one a donkey. I got the donkey. I always kidded everyone it was a jackass because my name was Jack. Seventy some years later these ornamental animals turn up every year on my sister Jean's Christmas tree. It is a little bit of 'nostalgia' from the past for us to treasure as a family.

I enjoyed, "Getting ready for Christmas," and each day leading up to Christmas I could see the delight in my three sisters' eyes. However once the tree was up and decorated, time itself seemed to stand still and Christmas was a long time in coming. I don't remember my sisters or me ever asking dad and mom for a certain gift. We didn't have great expectations. In fact in our everyday life we only had what was necessary and we each knew that asking for more would only be at the expense of the others.

We were encouraged to hang our socks on nails in the wall beside the old kitchen wood stove. In the morning we would be happy to find an apple, an orange and some homemade brown sugar and chocolate candy in the sock. If we were lucky there might be a homemade caramel popcorn ball or two.

As I got older I thought as a joke I would hang the biggest sock I could find which naturally was one of my dad's. When morning came, much to my delight I was greeted to huge bulging sock filled to capacity and for the moment I felt just a wee bit guilty for asking for soooo much. However once I removed the bag of candy and the orange I found an arrangement of apples, potatoes and even a small turnip in the toe. Santa, it seemed had a sense of humour. Early in my pre-teens I seemed to out-grow the need to hang my sock as I felt it was sissy, but my sisters would insist we all do this as a family tradition. So we continued as long as we were all at home.

One of the last things I would do on Christmas Eve was to put a burlap sack of nice green alfalfa or clover hay out by the hitching post in the yard for Santa's reindeer. My three sisters looked after Santa's lunch. Of course in the morning the hay was gone along with the milk and cookies. Yes Santa had come and gone. How much more proof did a kid need?

Early in the morning before dad and mom were up we would just have to take a peek to see if there really were gifts under the tree. There always were. I wonder how my dad and mom managed to do it, but they never failed.

On the farm you learn early in life, first things come first. Just because it was Christmas did not allow you time off from chores. The tree had to wait. There were cows to be fed and milked and perhaps a few newborn calves to pail feed. There were pigs to slop, hens to feed and above all we had to feed those horses.

I like to think that on Christmas day all the farm animals got just a wee bit more care and feed then usual. We would leave the barn with that feeling of contentment that we left all well and comfortable behind us.

When breakfast was over we gathered around the Christmas tree to open our presents. As always in those tough years there was just one special gift for each one of us. Then a few other smaller gifts which in time we were going to need anyway such as socks and mitts. Being kids we never thought of it that way. We just appreciated a gift and especially anything new.

Today I see kids tearing the wrap off an endless line of gifts, hardly stopping to acknowledge the gift they just opened before ripping the wrap off the next, and the next. I like to think in Christmas Past we were able to appreciate that special gift given to us and that we were both happy and more satisfied. The spirit of Christmas was both alive and well within us.

For Christmas dinner my dad would kill one of the few old red roosters that kept my mom's hens company. They thought they were king of the roost but unknown to them they would all eventually end up on the kitchen table for special occasions. I don't remember ever having turkey for Christmas until the forties when things on the farm got better. Mom was a great cook, thus our Christmas dinner was always the best. Each year my Grandma Cooke made a steamed English Christmas plum pudding and sauce. Because my grandma made it we had to eat it. Don't get me wrong the pudding was wonderful … just great ….but it arrived after I was full and ready to burst. That of course was not a good excuse for the family. Everyone had to eat Christmas pudding as it was a family tradition which was not to be broken.

I am comfortably retired now with many such memories stored away within me. However I have to realize that these are just that, "My Cherished Memories of Christmas past". They are also that of my sisters and those of my generation.

Memories for yet another generation will be made this Christmas and the next and the next and hopefully many years from now these young folk of today and tomorrow will have their own moments to reflect. A time when they to will sit in their retired years and contemplate their Christmases past.

Soft Water

A Soft Water Cistern

Good land and good water were two of the main ingredients the pioneers looked for in a new settlement. The first settlers clung to the rivers and ever-flowing creeks but very soon a well would be dug for drinking water near the house. The first pioneers no doubt had to use a wooden water bucket with a rope on it and bail for their water. In time a hand pump with a long handle would be installed. Later a few lucky souls had a windmill installed on the well near the barn to water the cattle while outside and for the other stock in the barn.

In Fullarton Township as in most of Ontario they found excellent drinking water almost everywhere but it was what they called hard water, which is water, containing a high level of calcium, magnesium, and other minerals. Hard water reduces the cleansing power of soap and leaves a lime-like deposit that makes your clothes very stiff. Those old fashioned bibbed overalls of grandpa's when washed in hard water would almost stand up in the corner of the kitchen all by themselves. Doing a large wash by hand with a scrub board in the tub was a hard task when you had to use the hard water from the well.

Thus next to digging a well for drinking water they set about building a cistern in the cellar to catch rainwater. This water was always referred to as soft water. Please note that I always hesitate to use the word basement while writing stories of those early years as people dug cellars, never a basement. The word basement came into use many years later. This cistern was filled with rainwater from off the house roof.

The size of the family or the size of your house would determine the size of the cistern. In pioneer days not everyone with a big family had a big house. However when it did rain you needed to catch as much rainwater as possible to tide you over the dry periods. I don't really remember our cistern ever going dry, however I do remember being able to skip a bath or two because the cistern was low in water. At the time I was very young and I didn't consider it an emergency at all. All this added up to the fact that we had more baths on a wet year then a dry year. Regardless, there was nothing more comforting on a rainy day than to listen to water flow into the cistern.

Most cisterns were dug down into the cellar floor a short way. I would reason that this was because most cellars were 7 feet deep so if you wanted to be able to see into your cistern then you had to leave a foot and a half or so of space at the top.
Then if you wanted a large, deep cistern you dug the footing of your cistern down deep into the cellar floor. This would also strengthen your cistern walls from the bottom up. Most cisterns were well made and lasted the lifetime of the farm home.

I understand the reason they seldom leaked was because a lot of chicken wire was put into the cement as a reinforcement to strengthen the walls. Then a special plaster or

mortar was used on the inside to keep it from leaking through porous cement. I have always heard it said that it is easier to hold water in than to keep it out.
I know it is true but I will let you figure that one out.

An overflow to a land drain was put in near the top of the cistern so it would not overflow into your cellar. Cisterns have a great history going back thousands of years as the Greeks and Romans used them in ancient history.

In the days of our pioneers all house roofs were shingled with cedar shingles. Getting water from the roof into the cistern was devised in a very simple way and made life ever so convenient for the household. Water ran down the roof into what they called the gutter a long trough that was attached to the face board at the bottom of the roof. The "trough" or gutter was sloped towards a down drain and that down drain ran the water into the cistern. Of course the water was unfit for drinking as sometimes leaves and dust and dirt and bird droppings were all washed away and ended up in your cistern.

There was also the odd mouse that fell in and could not climb out, thus there were times when we had to go fishing. Never mind we were very hardy souls born into a world that was less than perfect in some ways yet more earthly and never far from nature. Thus our cistern water always had a weak tea-like brackish colour to it, and it never smelled like roses. Even so with the use of a good soap all of your clothes turned out "Rinso White."

A wooden built-in water stand with a cast-iron sink was in place in the corner of our summer kitchen right above the cistern below. We marvelled at the convenience as it had a down drain into a bucket below. A small hand pump with a short handle was along side the sink. It seemed to me all those small pumps lost their prime when not in use every half hour or so. The large bucket that was in place below the sink would catch the used water. So water was used rather sparingly. The water was often left in the basin for the next person, and the next person to use. After the second or third person used it you could safely pour it down the drain without getting blessed for wasting water. Eh, small wonder I feel so close to my sisters.

When the bucket was full it was carried to the woodshed door and thrown out, for some reason always to the right never to the left. By spring it resembled the Sydney tar pond out there.

The reservoir on the rear of the kitchen wood stove would be kept full with soft water at all times. This became one of the first chores I had to do as a kid, " Fill the Reservoir".

To get some warm water to wash your hands and face you carried the washbasin from the sink to the stove and set it down on the rear stove plates. Then you lifted the lid on the reservoir and with the long handled dipper you dipped for the water you needed from the reservoir.

On Saturday nights a copper boiler would be placed on the front of the wood stove and filled with soft water. During the spring and summer months the round galvanized tub was placed in the wood shed just off the summer kitchen and in the winter for privacy the clothes horse was set up around the tub in a corner of the kitchen. None of this was thought of as being in anyway inconvenient as we never knew any difference. It was the way we were.

On Sundays we still felt very clean and it added meaning to the old saying of dressing up in your "Sunday Best". Actually most people had little choice of clothing as they only had one set of Sunday Best and it was kept freshly pressed for church, weddings and funerals or a very serious date.

It seemed the world around us got dustier and dirtier and the trees grew up surrounding the house with the branches extending out over the roof. Add the birds and bird dirt to the dust and grime and the need to be super clean the people gradually turned to water softeners and let the old cisterns go. The one on my dad's farm was under the back summer kitchen. When the summer kitchen was removed the cistern was filled with gravel and the lawn eventual extended over it.

There are times when I let my mind wander back to yesteryears to another time that I still hold dear. I hear that old kitchen pump being primed and I imagine my Saturday night bath is awaiting me in the woodshed.

While I wouldn't want to give up the conveniences I have today, I am grateful I experienced the journey from the woodshed and the summer kitchen to here. There is also the fact too that I wouldn't fit in that old tub very well anymore.

Wake Up

And

Smell The Coffee

Wake Up and Smell The Coffee

Actually there have been very few times in my life that I have had the pleasure of waking up to the smell of coffee. When I was very young children were not allowed to drink tea or coffee, as everyone knows it stunts the growth. Motherwell itself was a community of English and Scottish tea drinkers and growing up there I found myself surrounded by short stuff. When someone who was over 6 ft. tall came to church he got more attention than the minister. The average adult male at Motherwell stood not much more then five foot 8 or 10 inches in his stocking feet. I do suppose this was all because they drank black tea at least three times a day.

Coffee on the other hand was on the top shelf in the pantry and was saved for company. My mom had a small percolator with a strainer to hold the coffee at the top and a glass dome on the lid. First you had to build a wood fire in the kitchen stove large enough that would make the water in coffee pot boil. In time you would watch the water start to percolate, first very slowly and then gradually build up into a wild fury as it changed colour and pounded the glass top as if it were going to explode. In those days coffee smelled like coffee and it filled the house with its aroma. I am sure at that time they thought by boiling it long and hard they got all of the flavour out of the coffee, thus more for their money. A cup of coffee in those days seemed to be a potluck sort of thing. That is, while it smelled just wonderful sometimes it was glorious to drink and at other times it tasted as if someone had thrown in an old shoe.

The Scots and English went to great pains to make their tea but took little pride in knowing how to make a good cup of coffee.

My dad and mom drank several cups of tea at every meal, as did all of my grandparents, my uncles and aunts. Everyone in our family at that time was well under five foot eight or nine inches. My parents were determined that I could do better. So I was not allowed to drink tea or coffee until I was well into my teens. Perhaps I did a few times on the sly in defiance of my parents. Kids are like that. It's called, "Growing up."

In my prime I grew to an astounding height of five foot ten and a half inches.

One weekend away back in the 1940's my dad's sister, my Aunt Maude drove up from Detroit to the old farm for the weekend. She brought with her a jar of Nescafe. It was the first instant coffee I ever tasted. While it is 100 % coffee I never considered it real coffee but rather a new kind of drink I tried to like. Certainly it was convenient as it was fast to make. All you had to do was pour hot water over it, add your cream and sugar then stir and drink, but it didn't taste to me at all like coffee.

Very soon everywhere I ventured at home or in western Canada I ran into Nescafe. I learned to be polite and drink it but oh for a cup of real java. Thankfully most of my friends on the ranches in Alberta didn't accept it. They liked to make their coffee with real coffee the old fashioned way. They simply put the coffee in a coffee pot with no apparatus inside. They quickly brought the coffee to a good boil and then added a dash of cold water to make the grinds settle fast, then waited for one minute before serving. This was always good coffee. Of course as I always say, coffee with special friends just naturally tastes better.

For many years the coffee shops all over the country sported those tall stainless steel tanks with a glass tube up and down the front to show you how much coffee was left in the coffee maker. Early in the morning it was very good coffee but often this huge tank of coffee stood heated for hours and before the day was over was a sad imitation of the real thing. If you happened to arrive on the way home late at night you might receive one of the last few cups available. It would be black and strong and would all but make your hair stand on end. However for a time it seemed people just got used to bad coffee.

Over the years coffee has improved as new kinds of coffee makers were introduced. Today a good coffee maker can be found on almost anyone's kitchen counter. Thankfully a very good cup of coffee is no further away than the kitchen
I often associate the best coffee I have ever tasted with certain friends I have known. To this day I believe a certain beautiful French woman on a farm at Cypress River Manitoba made the best coffee in the world. Her name was Bertha Aubry. It was there I would wake up in the morning to the smell of coffee. It was during the Second World War and I was very young. I had gone west on what was called the harvest excursion to help the farmers get the grain crop harvested. I found out that the French drank coffee all day long. They drank it for breakfast, and dinner , supper and at bed time. They also took a large thermos to the field with them.

Next to Bertha Aubry's coffee I think I enjoyed the many cups of coffee I had at Don and Olive Sutherland's of Oyen Alberta. As much as the coffee I remember the many great conversations we had over those cups of coffee. It was there as a teen I came to realize my affection for ranch life. I never dreamed I would end up behind a barber chair in London Ontario.

As I grew older my fondness for a good cup of coffee seemed to increase. In my later years a Tim Hortons moved in across the street and my 5 foot ten and a half inches has shrunken a whole inch and a half. Need I explain anymore to you?

I do believe the best cups of coffee are those that you share with your family or friends, however there are times when you are alone that a good cup of coffee brings home to you a quiet comfort and a gathering of your thoughts.

A Family That Eats Together

A Family That Eats Together

There was a time when the whole family sat down to eat together every day. Even if the father was late doing chores in the barn or finishing working the land in a field at the back end of the farm, they waited. The table might be set but the food was kept warm at the back end of the wood stovetop until dad arrived.

The children knew and accepted it. No one could eat until dad was in his special armchair at the far end of the table. They learned not to whine about hunger, as it didn't work

When father finally arrived there was a welcome committee waiting for him inside the kitchen door. He probably thought his popularity was on the rise when the little wife and four very hungry growing kids greeted him so warmly.

While dad was washing himself up in the white galvanized washbowl in the old kitchen sink the food was placed on the table. Not one of us would dare to reach out to touch the food before my dad had sat down and the blessing was said. To do that was a no no, and a sign of disrespect, greed or selfishness. I learned early in life to share with my sisters as they did with me.

In our house we all had our assigned place at the table. My dad of course sat at the head of the table. No one else ever sat there and even when his armchair was not at the table it was recognized as his chair. To sit in it was more or less like a challenge to his clout. In our family dad was the head of the house, but we all knew that my mom held a trump card she used when she thought it was needed.

To dad's left sat my mom and next to her was Jean my youngest sister. I sat at the other end of the table facing my dad. Sister Pearl sat next to me on my left and then Laurine next to dad. We just never fought over who sat where as we just naturally wanted to be where we were.

fter dad said the grace, which always started out loud enough for us all to hear, "God bless," it quickly became inaudible, out of earshot. I had to sneak a look at him with one eye so as to know when to raise my head when it was over.

We didn't all reach out for food. We waited patiently for it to be passed to us. After that if you wanted seconds of something that was left you would say, "Please pass the carrots." Without a 'please' you might not get anything.

To start off the meal my mom would pass dad the potatoes, then the meat, then the vegetables. After she served him my dad would pass the food to his right, never to the left. My mom always waited until last. At the time I don't think my sisters or I gave this much thought, as it was my parent's design for mealtime. However I do think about it today as often in the thirties there were times that there was no more than just enough to go around. I like to think that it was mom's special way of teaching us to share.

Of course those little things like table manners were taught to us without us realizing it. When everyone sits down at the table together parents are better able to observe their children's table manners and do something about it. Later in life your children will thank you, as it's hard to go out and about in this world with no table manners and feel at home.

We were expected to understand a few basic table manners, it goes like this - (Don't take more food than you can eat. Don't talk with your mouth full. Close your mouth when you eat. Sit up when you're at the table. Use your knife and fork. Don't pick at your food. Don't mush your food. Never get the sugar spoon wet. Turn your head when you sneeze or cough and above all get your elbows off the table.)

This last one seemed to be important although I'm sure had anything to do with good table manners. But it was the law. The one I hated the most was if you don't eat up your liver and onions then you can't have any dessert.

I still don't eat liver and onions.

When TV came into our lives it seemed parents let their children eat in front of the TV. Thus now several generations later it has become natural to go to the kitchen and take a plate of food to the living room and eat it in front of the TV.

There is no "Thank You" for the food, no grace or blessing said, no sense of sharing, no table manners and no family conversations. It is very much like feeding a flock of hungry hens in your living room three times a day.

I realize times have changed and many people work on shifts. Often both the father and mother are working. All this has damaged the old family tradition of everyone being able to be at the table at the same time, a special time together.

There is an old saying that a family that eats together stays together. I do believe it helps to make close family ties.

The family today is very much more privileged in the line of entertainment and travel than ever before. On any given night dad or mom may be working on a shift and Johnny might have to play baseball at suppertime, and Jane may have to go to the Y for swimming lessons. Mealtime it seems has had to become flexible.

For the modern parents today it seems they must weigh the benefits of a great social life for the family afield against the loss of a healthy family life at home.

The other night I was watching the 6 o-clock news and they were interviewing a family who claimed they were trying something new. Every night they all sat down at the table together for supper. The mother said she found that her kids ate a better balanced meal instead of one or two things. The father said he found it a good time to find out just what his kids were thinking about. When they interviewed the children, the children said they liked it as they enjoyed their food better sitting at the table with good conversation.

So have faith, as this is a hard one for active families today. Regardless of what they do, or try to do, in their hearts they know good table manners never go out of style.

A Wondrous Gift

A Wondrous Gift

Two Little Fawns

Do you believe that there are times in life, when you may witness something, you can't explain to others, - something so pure, so wondrous that it will stay with you all the years of your life?

In your heart you have this strange feeling that just for the moment or for a few minutes God granted you a gift, of a wondrous vision of beauty that would be yours to keep for as long as you live. That is what happened to me.

When I was perhaps 10 or 12 years old, I was awakened in the night because of the brilliant light shining in the bedroom window. I looked out over the veranda roof of the second story window of the old farmhouse into the little field between the house and the road. There I saw the most beautiful shafts of moonbeams coming down from all sides between the rows of spruce trees, which edged in the little field. The moonbeams seemed to be setting a stage for the perfect central scene... Then, to the orchard side beneath the spruce I saw two fawns emerge very slowly and cautiously into the shafts of moonbeams. It was as if the beauty of that wondrous light that surrounded them enchanted them too. Soon they felt safe and they began to dance, to jump and run amid the moonbeams.
How can I describe it to you? It was heavenly. I know I witnessed something special that night. The next morning I tried to tell my dad and mom about it, but I know they felt it was just a kid's dream, but I knew it was for real.

At this time of my life I know there were other times that I now look back to with wonder. How is it that days, weeks and years can go fleeting by without any memorable times or moments and then suddenly there are these special moments that many years later you reflect back to with clarity?

I can think of several and each time I had the feeling I had just witnessed something. I was aware it was a shared experience I was not alone.

My Dad And The Butcher Knife

My Dad and The Butcher Knife

My dad often had to fill in for my mom while she was at the Women's Institute meeting at the Motherwell United Church. It seems occasionally while trying to save all the little kids in China they had to stay late at the church for supper. Actually, the ladies came well prepared to stay for a long, long time in their good old-fashioned way with a potluck supper. Soon steaming bowls of heavenly food were on the table and perhaps for dessert one of Mrs. Nairn's masterpieces, which was a dark chocolate cake.

Meanwhile back home on the farm, dad would come in from doing the early evening chores to find four hungry kids on his hands. Each kid was just as hungry as any little kid in China, or so it seemed to dad. My dad was self-taught in his very own ways of survival and he never changed in a lifetime. He would head straight to the knife drawer in the old kitchen cabinet and out came that old magic Butcher Knife. None of us was allowed to touch it! We all knew there was something very special about a Butcher Knife. It was not a thing for kids to handle. To tell the truth we didn't give a lot of thought as to why, for in those days kids did as they were told and asked few questions. One thing we did know was my dad could work wonders with a Butcher Knife and nothing else to get a whole meal.

My mom made those wonderful large round loaves of homemade bread, yeasty in flavour and spongy to the touch, with an aroma my sisters and I would gladly die for today. With his Butcher Knife dad would slice the whole loaf and then place it on the table without a plate. My mom would never do this so we thought it was, as kids would say today, "real cool."

Then there was a large bowl of homemade butter, which we kids helped to make by taking turns shaking cream in a large jar. The cream of course came from our very own cows, with old Boots and Bessie being kindly thought of.

Next we all followed dad with the Butcher Knife into the cool unheated front hall where on the floor sat a huge round wooden cheese box made of elm thinly sliced from great elm logs right there at the local box factory in Fullarton Village. The box was made to hold three large round cheeses, each about four inches high and eighteen or twenty inches across. The cheese was made in the Stacy cheese factory right next door to the box factory. Beside the cheese box sat a full-size cream can, which in the fall was filled with local honey. We all loved to sneak into the hall with dad and the Butcher Knife, as when he sliced off generous pieces of cheese or a large curl of honey there were always a few small pieces for us.

Of course when mom was home we were not to tell her as it was called piecing before mealtime, and that was a no, no, but I'm sure my mom knew all about it.

The Butcher Knife worked well in the cream can too, and soon large golden curls of honey filled a bowl. Then we would follow dad and the Butcher Knife back to the kitchen where dad lit the coal oil lamp and soon a warm glow settled over the kitchen table. Dad would have his tea and my sisters and I would fill our glasses with our own milk.

Then we gathered around the table in the glow of the lamplight, knowing enough not to touch anything until the blessing was said, "We thanked the Lord for this his blessing, and for dad and the Butcher Knife, and please God don't forget those starving little kids in China".

While there was always a shortage of cash I never remember being hungry. There were always homemade scones and tea biscuits on hand in our kitchen and a fresh chocolate cake every weekend. My mom was a good cook and I know she worked hard to see that we didn't know hunger. But just the same I was aware many people did know hunger - especially all those little kids in China, so I always had to clean up my plate, no matter how full I was. "Eat it up; the little kids in China are starving."

Oh yes, I worked hard to save a lot of little kids in China. We thanked the Lord for this his blessing, and for dad and the Butcher Knife, and please God don't forget those starving little kids in China.

Home-Made Bread

252

Home Made Bread

"Bread Is The Staff of Life."

I have fond memories of my mom's homemade bread. In those years of the great depression of the 1930's homemade bread was the usual, as you would find it in every home in the country. Every young girl worth her salt had to know how to bake bread. There was a saying, "First think of the bread then of the bride."

In those days it was important that a girl's mother have a great recipe for bread.

There are few things as tantalizing as walking into the kitchen just as the bread is ready to come out of the oven. While hot bread is hard to slice it is well worth the effort. Butter melts almost instantly as you spread it over the hot yeasty bread.

A slice of cheese would be just right. Most people found no need for jam or jelly.

There has always been a sort of mystery surrounding the making of homemade bread and I know it has mostly to do with what they call the, "First Starter". In those early days they didn't use a commercial yeast to make the bread rise.

This first starter was carefully prepared made from pure well water and stone ground wheat. It seems very clean non-treated stone ground wheat flour was mixed with pure well water (that means no chlorine). When mixed two proteins called glutamine and gliaden are transformed into what is called gluten which chain traps bubbles created in the yeast, this causes the bread to rise. This starter, once made is kept in a crock in the pantry and added to the bread when it was made. The starter was fed fresh flour each time some was used so that it would keep on growing.

The starter is yeast and is considered to be a live single cell or microorganisms that live on the products in the flour. More simply put yeast is small things whose food is mostly sugar found in the flour and whose waste products are carbon dioxide and alcohol. The yeast is active at 5 C, its rate of growth increases with the temperature up to 38 C. If the temperature increases to 40 C. the yeast is killed. It is best kept at 35C.

To create good bread it was better to make a large batch at one time as the yeast would cause more rise in a large batch of dough and make better bread.

There are perhaps three things I remember most about watching my mom make bread. The first was a large granite enamel bread pan that hung on the pantry wall. The second was a hand turned flour sifter. For some reason it seemed all flour had to pass through the sifter and little bits of "whatnots" filtered out.

When the desired amount of flour was in the pan, water and salt were added at the centre. To start off she mixed from the centre with a large spoon until the batter became too heavy to stir. At this point mom would knead the flour with her hands always from the outside towards the centre. If needed she would add more water as she worked her way to the outer edge of the pan. If by chance it became too sticky she picked up the flour sifter and added a sift of flour over the dough and kneaded it in. It had to be just right so it all held together and yet not stick to the pan.

As a rule she did this on the kitchen table late in the evening just before we kids were sent off to bed. The bread pan with the dough was left covered with a cloth cover overnight in the kitchen.

The next morning my sisters and I would all be amazed at what had happened overnight to the batch of dough in the pan; it was simply magical. The kitchen itself had a pleasant scent; a yeasty smell and the dough had risen to double its height in the pan creating a dome in the center.

At this point the dough had to be punched down until it was about the same size it was the night before. This was what they called the second rising.

Again it was covered and left to rise in a warm area of the kitchen. This second rising usually only takes a short time.

Mom had to tell us not to touch it or to uncover it while she was off to the barn to help with the milking. For small kids it was tantalizing to have to wait until breakfast was over and the dishes and cream separator washed before mom could get started at the bread.

Now is the time to introduce that third thing I said I remembered about mom and her bread. She had a very large bread baking board especially made for bread. It too was kept in the pantry. It was made of beautiful yellowed natural wood and about 36 in. wide times 30 inches deep with a 3 ½ inch board on both sides and the back. It was always spotlessly clean. It was placed on the table next to the bread pan.

First she lightly floured the breadboard and then mom would reach for the dough and pull a handful out and with the butcher knife expertly cut just the right amount off. It always appeared to cut off in a diamond wedge shape. She would cut off perhaps four or six pieces before she would start to knead a loaf of bread.

It was amazing to watch her endlessly knead the dough with the knuckles and the heel of the hand always turning it into its self. When it felt just right she rounded it and shaped it into a loaf and popped it into a bread pan. One after the other the slabs of dough were grabbed and kneaded and placed in the bread pans.

The loaves were then covered with a cloth again and left to rise in a warm area of the kitchen.

I only remember round homemade loaves of bread. I don't remember long loaves being made on the farm like the ones they sold in the Bake Shops.

In time the old wood fired cook stove would be fed wood to make a hot fire so the oven temperature would be just right at the time the bread was to be baked.

I watched my mom make bread many times. I know that there is a lot of hard work involved, but that was a part of farm life in the thirties. To day it is almost a lost art. Real homemade bread is nothing like the bread from the bread making machines we have today. It is however a teasing, fragrant, tantalizing reminder of the real thing.

For much of the 1930's there was very little store bought bread or pastry in most of the country's farm homes. However there were all kinds of homemade pies and cakes and muffins, and always lots of fresh and preserved fruit.

I find it hard to believe now but my mom would often put a pie and cake on the table along with a large bowl of fruit. All of this was home made. The fruit could be wild raspberries from our bush picked by my sisters and me, or it might be pears or applesauce from our orchard.

In the 1940's things started to get better down on the farm and there was a bit more money to spend on things that at that time were considered luxuries.

I remember my mom's brother my Uncle Bob Butson got a job delivering bread for a bakery in Mitchell. His route took him out of town as far as our place. He drove a panel truck that had wooden rack shelves across the back behind the cab and there were shelves down each side. This was I think about the time my mom stopped making homemade bread. I would think the reason for this was two fold. She was tired of making so many loaves of bread and then too she wanted to help her brother sell bread.

When he arrived in our yard we would all go out to greet him. My sisters and I would gather close to the rear doors of the truck anxious to not only see but to smell the bread and all the goodies he brought. Besides the bread there was all kinds of pies and cakes, several kinds of buns and muffins. My mouth did water.

I remember how neat it looked when uncle Bob took a long pole like a broom handle with a bent nail in the end and with a quick motion of his wrist make the bread fly off the rack and end up next to him at the doors. He carried a huge leather pouch strapped around his waist, which was full of money from the day's sales.

This bakery in Mitchell made wonderful donuts and chelsea buns. It seems at the end of the day there were often a few things left over. Many times Uncle Bob handed my mom a pack of chelsea buns or donuts saying they were stale when I am sure they were not. To us country kids they were a touch of heaven. To this day every time I see chelsea buns I think of my Uncle Bob and his kindness.

Bread at that time was about 10 cents a loaf. I know that sounds cheap but that's not so. Consider that a gallon (not a litre) of gasoline cost about 25 cents and a hired man on the farm might earn $25.00 a month with room and board. A factory worker could earn a dollar a day for a ten-hour day, which is ten cents an hour.

Quotations

In hard times it was said, "Half a Loaf is better than none at all."

When the young man got a good job he was, "The Breadwinner" of the family.

If he made a lot of money they said, "He has a Lot of Dough."

When he lost his job he had to, "Join The Bread Line."

Bread is known worldwide and respectably mentioned far back in history.

Bread is one of the world's oldest basic foods.

It is said bread feeds not only the body but it also feeds the soul.

Memories of Other Times

Memories of Other Times

My Grandmother's Family "The Collins"

My Great Grandfather, George Edwin Collins was born in England in 1815. He was one of 8 children, 4 boys and 4 girls. He was the son of a well-to-do carriage-maker. Upon the death of his parents the business was sold to the oldest brother. Then three of the brothers one of whom would one day be my great grandfather and one sister Elizabeth and her husband Joseph Bennett left England for the American colony.

They were an industrious family of many trades from blacksmith, iron and forge workers, to the carpenters trade and cabinetmakers. They also knew brick laying and a bit about farming. They first settled in New York City area in early 1830's during the cholera outbreak. They found immediate work because of their skills in carpentry and cabinet making. They were hired to make coffins. While the money was good the risk of death was all about them so after a time they heeded the governments urge to, go west young man, go west.

They moved first to Virginia and then to Detroit where they helped to build some of the very first brick buildings in Detroit. Perhaps because of their accent and fresh from England appearance they felt uncomfortable in the U S. There was still much unrest between the United States and Britain. Most of the Collins family decided to cross the Detroit River to a place called Maidstone Crossing, ten miles out of Windsor. That is the place where my grandmother was born, Maidstone.

My Grandma and Her Sisters.
In 1866 George Edwin Collins and his wife Sarah (Nicholson) Collins moved their family to a farm in East Zorra Township of Oxford County near Woodstock. I have often wondered how and why they strayed north to Woodstock while the rest of the Collins family stayed down south close to their Canadian roots.

Aunt Maimie whose real name was Mary Jane never married. The two sisters lived in houses side by side in Woodstock. Aunt Lizzie, whose real name was of course Elizabeth married a John Grimstead who died in 1904 at the age of 75.

My grandmother by chance met my grandfather George Cooke who at 21 years of age was fresh out of England in 1887 and was farming a rented piece of land somewhere southwest of Woodstock. While he could drive a horse and milk a cow, grow grain and make hay he couldn't fry an egg or make a decent spot o tea. So naturally he was looking for a wife. He married my grandmother Alice P Collins in March of 1892.

Three children were born to them while they farmed that farm near Woodstock. George, Bertha and John. John of course was my dad born in October 21st. 1898. The fourth child, my Aunt Alice Maude, was born later.

My Grandfather George Edward Cooke

In 1899 my Grandfather set out in his horse and buggy to look for a farm he might buy north of St Marys on the Mitchell Road near the village of Motherwell.

Alex Bothwell was the owner of the farm at that time. I am sure my grandfather was thrilled by what he saw. There was a brand new huge white brick house with several gable ends and a built on summer kitchen and woodshed. This was sure to please my grandmother. Then there was a large hemlock sided barn and a drive-in-shed with an attached hen house. Grandpa first rented it and then later bought the farm. It was 162½ acres. He lived there the rest of his life. I never knew him to take more then an overnight holiday until he died of cancer in 1941. Sad as it was he never got a chance to make even one trip back to his home in England.

Woodchips from the Woodpile

In those early days every active farm had a wood yard, where wood from the bush was stored and made ready for the kitchen stove or the furnace. Eventually, with hard work every wood yard got turned into a chip yard. The wood yard for convenience would be beside --- near --- or at the back of the house. Every farm kitchen had a great old-fashioned wood cook stove where the meals were cooked. Some smaller houses had a pot bellied stove to heat the house during the cold winter months. These pot-bellied stoves had a smoke (stack) pipe running up to the ceiling into the centre of the bedroom above, then across the room to a hole in the wall where it entered the chimney. This was usually on the gable end of a house. This stove pipe gave off just a hint of heat, or enough so the chamber pot under the bed didn't freeze over.

If you were one of the lucky ones you might have a huge old grate shaking type furnace in the cellar that ate up large blocks of wood day and night and spewed out equal ashes. For a time it did give off a lot of heat. It was usually all or none at all.

My grandfather spent many hours in the wood yard on the west side of the house with his favourite axe, splitting blocks of hard wood maple, elm and beech. He was an expert at it. He knew a good block of wood when he saw one and I am sure he had a sort of affection for it as a thing of beauty. He knew just where the block would split clean across the grain and then cut clean again and again. Firewood had to be cut just so into smaller pieces, for the kitchen wood stove to build a small fast fire. Then for our furnace it would be split into larger pieces.

To cook every meal in the heat of mid summer you had to light a fire in the kitchen stove. To avoid overheating the kitchen you would keep on hand what they called kindling, small cut wood that was dry and makes a quick fire without a lot of lasting heat from the stove in the kitchen. Every mother had to know how to start a fire in the kitchen stove.

In his later years it became grandpa's job to split wood and he spent many hours out there. I like to think he did it leisurely, as I am sure he enjoyed it as a retreat from other jobs that had been much harder on him. I remember watching him with great concern for you see I was sure one of those days he was going to split his foot.

He would first split a large block into several pieces and then lay one piece down flat on the ground. He then leaned the other up onto it and placed his foot on the bottom of the sloped piece of wood and whacked it neatly with the sharp axe-blade. He proceeded to cut it into several nice size pieces that would fit together comfortably in the kitchen cook stove. He did all this with great care. The chips would fly in every direction and litter the yard and there in lies my story.

The great blocks of wood piled outside the woodshed door in time would all fall under my grandpa's axe, kindling, stove wood, and split blocks for the furnace and above all lots and lots of great hardwood chips.

My grandma would often appear at the woodshed door and with great care come down the tall woodshed steps to chat with grandpa. Before going back into the house she would load her apron with nice fresh clean woodchips. Woodchips were considered a bonus and were the very best for starting a fire in the stove.

My Grandmother's Two Sisters

My grandma's two sisters Aunt Maimie and my Aunt Lizzy would come two or three times a year and spend a week with my grandparents on the farm. As a kid I always enjoyed having company as our farm was far out in the country and life gets a bit boring being raised with three sisters. However in this case I think I suffered from some sort of lapse of memory or else I loved the punishment.

Still, I remember them kindly as two very set and very strict, God fearing little old ladies.

We were happy to see them come but even more than happy to see them go. When they came to visit my Grandma they thought they had the divine right to order us kids about. At that time it was thought all kids were here on earth to serve their elders. They just could not stand to see idle hands, as they were sure the devil would find work for us. The water bucket had to be kept full to the brim. The garden could be weeded and then weeded again. The lawn grass kept cut, anything to keep us busy. When all else was done they had you picking up chips from the wood yard.

At that time all wood fruit baskets were either 12 or 6-quart baskets. Every kid in the country knew what gathering chips meant. The basket of woodchips was placed behind the kitchen stove to dry. These dry chips were in great demand to start a quick fire on cool fall mornings or to begin a fire at mealtime. Working hard to get the job done was not an option while my two dear old aunts were visiting. Just when I had the baskets full of woodchips and thought I was done out the door would come my dear old aunty with more baskets and nary a kind work or any praise. Child labour was very much in style and needed. It was in tune with the times and was the standard way of raising a good kid. Don't knock it because I am a product of the system. .... Solid Gold.

I also remember they often had us pick baskets of plantain leaves. Plantain is a broad leaf plant and is a common weed found in areas near the barnyard. They would line their shoes with leaves to relieve foot pain. Apparently the leaves had some medicinal value. *(I learned years later it is recognized as a herb and very good for treating cuts and abrasives.)*

Years ago shoes were bought from a cobbler or just any local store. Many of these shoes did not fit a foot comfortably when first bought. There was not much thought given to the idea of buying a shoe that fit. It was thought you had to break them in and **make** them fit. They just went out and bought a good sturdy, sensible shoe. Many ordered out of a catalogue. Almost everyone suffered from bunions and sore feet from time to time.

Death In The Family
My Aunt Mamie died of gangrene in Woodstock March 17th. 1934. Perhaps it is not a good idea to introduce death to children so young as perhaps they don't understand the

finality of death, and it is very hard for parents to explain it or justify it to children. Yet I cannot say it was wrong as otherwise I would not have the memories I have.

I remember my Grandma Cooke going down to Woodstock and staying with her sister for some time, - or until the end.

I remember my dad driving down in our model A Ford taking us all as a family for one last visit to see our dear old Aunt Maimie. As children I don't think we understood death. It was something that only grown ups talked about. Children were not expected to understand or question it.

I was just five years old coming six in the fall. Because of Aunt Mamie's illness my mom had packed a lunch for us at dinnertime. At noon we drove downtown in Woodstock and parked on a lot with a large water fountain that threw water up into the air then fell back into the area below. There were many pigeons flying about and drinking from the fountain.

Up until that day I had never tasted any kind of pop. Dad left the car and sometime later came back with a large bottle of bubbly stuff. At the time I had no idea what it was. It was ginger ale. However when I raised it to my face I inhaled and the darn stuff entered my nose and it hurt. I somehow connected this bubbly stuff to the water in that fountain and since the pigeons were bathing in it I decided it was not fit to drink anyway.

After dinner we went back to the house to visit. It was not the kind of visit children enjoy. The house was dark and it smelled strange

Aunt Maimie may have lived for many years if she had not being so stubourn. Having much pride she would not let them take the gangrene infected leg off so she suffered a long and painful death. I remember my Grandmother putting garlic in tin cans on top of hot wood coals in the corners of each room; it was supposed to kill the smell and the germs. At the time they feared the disease and thought they might catch it too.

Aunt Maimie died March 17th 1934 and in 1937. In Aunt Lizzy sold her house and moved to 1184 Hall Street in the city of Windsor and lived with her daughter Em. Aunt Lizzy passed away Nov. 26th 1947. My grandfather passed away in the spring of 1941. After a lengthily illness, with cancer, he died at home in his own bed.

My Grandmother Cooke lived on for ten more years or until Oct. 27th. 1951

Tip

To Insure

Promptness

TIP

To Insure Promptness

Growing up in rural Ontario I never had to worry about tipping anyone. I was aware some older people left a dime or two for the waitress when they left the table after finishing a meal, but it was not expected of youth. The truth is I was never to a restaurant with my dad and mom all the years I was growing up on the farm. It just seemed that my three sisters and myself plus dad and mom made six and eating out was not an option as it was not affordable.

As I grew older and left home I sometimes left a small tip when I could afford it and the food and service was extra good. Still most people didn't leave a tip for just a cup of coffee as they feel they must do today when served coffee at a table.

Someone has to pay the server, but ask yourself, "Should that someone be you?"

The first time I ever gave much thought to "Tipping" and what it really looked like was a few weeks after I started school at Droulard's Barber College in Windsor.

On the second day of school in Jan. 1963 we were told we were going to do our very first haircut with hand clippers. We all wondered though just how we were going to get our first head of hair into our barber chair for that very first haircut.

Thus enters Mr. Droulard the owner of Droulard's Barber College who in a loud voice to a room full of longhaired kids says,

"Who of you would like a nice free hair cut?" about a dozen kids all put their hands up and shouted "Me!"

"Go down the stairs and into the classroom."

We all followed the kids down the stairs into a long narrow basement room where a dozen empty barber chairs sat waiting. The kids all scampered aboard anxious to save themselves 35 cents. Little did they know what was about to happen, as to the kids we all looked very much like real barbers in our freshly starched white uniforms.

Mr. Droulard went from chair to chair handing out hand clippers. Some of the children looked at the hand held clippers and let out a moan. Mr. Droulard put his hand on top of his hapless victims head bowing it and then started clipping up the back of the kid's neck. The hair fell in an orderly manner in great locks; first curling and then rolling down his clipper hand and finally fell silently to the floor. He quickly and expertly did the back and then both sides. Then he stood back admiring his work. He invited us to take our clipper in hand and do the same.

I must admit these kids were either very brave or very foolish and all for 35 cents. Soon great clumps of hair were falling as clippers ran wild and deep. Sometimes too deep and some kid would shout, "Ouch, that's my ear."

In the end it was not a pretty sight. There were buckets of not too clean hair on the floor and kids with scruffy looking haircuts and great red welts up and down their necks. Soon however two teachers came to the rescue and added a few personal touches so in the end the poor kid thought he got a decent haircut. The kids were let out the side door so they could not mingle with those in the waiting room on the main floor. The kids we had just cut rushed off to spend their money. Again Mr. Droulard asked the crowd in the waiting room,

"Who all wants a free hair cut?" "Go down the stars to the class room." We would go through it all again. * From the book, Getting By In A Silent World, by Jack L Cooke

Within a few weeks some of us started to do very good haircuts and we started to get repeat customers. It was then that I noticed some of the young lads working hard for a TIP.

We had been told of course to be friendly and courteous to all of our customers, but we had never been told to work for TIPS, or how to handle it. I began to see some of the boys take the haircloth off their customer and then vigorously start to brush their shoulders for hair on their shirt or jacket. Hair that just was not there.

The guys followed the customer all the way to the door never letting up on small talk and the brushing. It was very obvious and easy to see they were working very hard for a tip; they all but put their hand out. What they didn't seem to understand was that it made them and the whole trade school appear <u>cheap.</u>

In my mind's eye I can still see the guys following the customer all the way to the door brushing them vigorously. That is how I remember a small number of those students to this day, cheap; they sold their pride for a T I P

At the Barber College the clientele was mostly school kids and young college students and they paid for their haircut in advance at the door as they came in.

I too was very much short of cash while going to barber college but I just could not bring myself to do that. When I was offered a tip I was very uncomfortable about it, as I felt the haircut had already been paid for at the door.

When I cut your hair you cannot buy a better haircut from me, as I will always give you the best cut I can. Tipping me won't get a better haircut. Also it won't get you into the chair any sooner. Good shops will not juggle customers.
Yes I did take tips later in my own shop, but never without first saying,

"No you don't have to do that."

I tried to make it very clear to everyone in my clientele that all I needed from them was to be a good steady customer and that I would charge them the average going price for a haircut. I never charged the most money in town for a haircut and certainly never the least.

I feel I can speak out re tipping because I worked for 40 years in the service line.

I would like to say if ever there is a time for a tip it might be perhaps if you catch the barber leaving for lunch or closing his door to go home and he re-opens the shop just for you. Or perhaps you have been away on holidays and you have twice the amount of hair to cut.

In my case I would go to the hospital or make a house call for a <u>steady customer</u> and not charge him any extra. I like to think of it as Red Green on TV says,

"We're all in this together, so I'm pulling for you"

I would tell them if you're in my clientele and you come to me while you're in good health I will go to you when you're ill or in the hospital at no extra charge.

What is in a tip and how it get started,

The definition given for a tip is that it is a **gratuity,** a small amount of money given **voluntarily** in appreciation for service rendered. The word TIP itself comes from the words, "To Insure Promptness"

Some say it started out in England where feudal landlords threw small coins from their carriage into the street to peasants when they ventured in the street to ensure themselves safe passage. Others believe it started in the village pub where men sought to show off their prestige by tipping the server better to ensure he got better service than those around him. He thought, that **this** made him a somebody.

Last week I went out for supper with two friends at a very nice little place on Oxford Street here in London. I ordered my favourite ... roast beef and I was to have a salad with French dressing and a glass of water now and my coffee later.
I was also to get rice pudding along with the meal.

The meal arrived, that is my roast beef arrived and truly when I saw it I forgot all about the salad that went along with the meal. We never saw the waitress until she brought the bill. It was then I asked her about the salad and the coffee. She said she was, "Sorry"....... She asked me about the rice pudding but I declined as everyone else had finished eating. So we set about dividing the bill.

Everyone at the table shelled out generously to T I P that waitress even myself. I cannot but ask, "Why did I, and why do we, do it?" If tipping is not for good service, then what is it for? Is it just because we know it is expected of us and we cannot leave the table with a clear conscience unless we pay? I am sure we all are aware that giving our support to this system is never going to solve the minimum wage problem.

Lets be honest here - Is it just the fact we don't want to appear cheap to our friends or dining company? Thus we often tip regardless of the service rendered and all too often more than we can afford...out of guilt, but I can't quite understand why. We do not want to anger the server even though he or she failed to serve us? Perhaps if the food was good we might want to come back again and bring a friend. Most servers have good memories and we don't want an unpleasant server.

It used to be considered ok to TIP 10% of your bill and now even though food costs us a lot more thus the bill is much larger they complain the average TIP is only 15% and they want 20% from the public who largely work for wages and are already taxed to death. Also I wonder how much of the tipping industry is tax-free? You must remember tipping is a multi million-dollar industry on the backs of the working public.

Senior citizens are now the largest part of Canadian society. I have often wondered why we don't band together and do something about this tipping problem. Let us say as a group; ok if you expect us to help you pay the wages of your staff then give us a free cup of coffee with our meal, or tie the tip to a free second cup of coffee. When you look at the menu they put up a fair front with a price on a meal. However the shock comes when they add up your bill. There is $2.00 for a coffee and in many places a charge again for the second cup of coffee.

The meal that you thought you could afford has suddenly jumped $5.00 with the extra cost for coffee. Then there are still provincial and federal taxes to pay, and you are still expected to T I P fifteen or twenty percent on top of all this to the server. Not all of us can afford it. We have worked hard all our lives and feel that we owe it to ourselves to eat out now and then. I am sure thousands of people would eat out more if they could afford it. The restaurants seem blind to the fact that they are sitting on a golden egg as we seniors all get older, but that egg **ain't** going to hatch unless they make changes.

The tipping I have written about here is only the petty stuff. That is tipping the waiter or waitress or the barber the hairdresser and the hairstylist, the paperboy and the pizza deliveryman, but lets think big -

If you really want to feel the pain then take a trip abroad or even out of town for a week end.

If you stop at a hotel the bellhop will grab your luggage and he expects to be paid by the number of bags you have plus taking into account how heavy they are. He will expect a couple of dollars for each bag The car valet will take your car away and park it and when you want it he will bring it back and expect two to five dollars for his service.

If you're staying for a second or more days the maid will expect five to ten dollars a day to put your room back in order. It depends on how much you messed it up.

If you have dinner in the hotel restaurant you will have to leave a tip of fifteen to twenty percent for the server and if you order a bottle of wine you may have to pay a tip of fifteen or twenty percent on the cost of the wine to the wine steward to open and serve the wine. They will keep telling you the better you pay the better the service. Thank you, very much but I think I will stay closer to home.

There was a time it was hard to keep your shop open just cutting hair. I never gave thought to earning tips above the cost of a haircut. I thought I needed more heads of hair. When that didn't come I took a second job as custodian of an office building to supplement my income. Then along came a third part time job of cutting hair two nights a week at a boy's residential college.

When I worked at several jobs for many years to make ends meet and make it possible to have some savings it seemed completely out of character for me to throw my hard-earned money away to others who could possibly do the same. Most of these people were better able to help themselves than I was as I was deaf.

However it seems we would rather follow the crowd like lemmings in a self-destructive way and not rock the boat. When else do people pay additional money for a service they have already paid for without negotiating the amount up front?

The industry thrives on greed and as long as people willingly support it, it will continue to thrive.

One

Cold Winter's Day

In St. Marys

274

One Cold Winter's Day In St. Marys

It was in early to mid 1930's and I was in St.Marys sitting alone in the back seat of the old model A Ford about mid way down the north side of the block, facing west towards the bridge and the Thames River. As time went by my feet started to tingle and then of course my fingers and then my hands and even my nose. I had known it was going to be a long cold wait alone in the car, and even under the buffalo robe the cold was sinking in. Nevertheless I had insisted as I didn't want to be dragged from store to store while my dad and mom shopped for things that only grown ups would buy. It was my mom who invented the old saying shop till you drop.

Don't get me wrong, it was not that she had a purse full of money to spend it was more to do with spending her few dollars wisely. She would check out the stuff in several dry good stores for the best goods at the best price and them gladly walk across town to save a few pennies. At the time I didn't understand but now I know she did what she had to.

The winters of the 1930's were arctic cold, and even at a tender age of perhaps five or six years old I knew what it was like to be cold. My sisters and I played in the snow banks that encircled our farm buildings for hours on end. These banks were caused by the endless winds that drove the snow across the fields and howled about the farm buildings and piled the snow higher and higher into long wonderfully mountainous curved banks some times six and seven and more feet high. Often we played for hours while our toes grew numb and our feet froze and the lobes of our ears grew pink then white in the cold. We knew very early in life what frostbite felt like. We considered a little bit of frostbite nothing unusual. It was something we lived on the edge with every day during the winter. We played hard to keep our body heat up so as to keep warm.

Most children wore wool gloves or mitts that eventually got wet and ended up on the oven door to dry awaiting our next outing. In the evenings it was not unusual to smell scorched wool on the oven door and the faint aroma of kindling drying within the oven of most farm kitchen stoves.

Sometimes we covered out ears with our bare hands to defrost them so we could stay out and play in the snow just a wee while longer. In the end the cold always won as it forced us indoors. Often we had frozen fingers and ear lobes long before we realized it as it crept upon us slow like. The real pain came when we went inside and started to thaw out.

Of course our parents would scold us for not having enough sense to come in out of the cold, but when you're a kid having fun, what adults call common sense, does not apply.

The truth was we didn't have the kind of winter clothing that the kids have today so when you went outside we expected that in time we would eventually get cold and have to go in. It was a part of winter. You soon learned not to stand around idle, keep on the move, play hard and keep warm.

As for me the longer I sat in the old Model A car the colder I got. While children might be left alone in the car or on a buggy we were told to sit tight and not get out of the car and wander the street.

In the winter in those days there was little comfort as far as warmth, no matter how you traveled. Still traveling by car was a far cry from riding all the way into town and home again in an open sleigh or cutter. At that time not all of the early cars even had a heater. At the best some cars offered a hot water heater installed low under the dash on the passenger side. The person sitting on the passenger side directly in front of the heater had toasted legs and feet while the children in the back snuggled together under a buffalo robe trying to keep their feet off the cold floor to keep them from freezing, but such was life.

So there I was all alone and freezing to death in the back seat of our model A and I had no one to blame but myself. If I had the brains of my sisters I would be inside some nice warm store right now probably looking at bolts of cloth or needles and thread with mom. My mom was always buying a piece of this and a piece of that and turning it into an apron for herself or the church bazaar, or else she cut it all into small pieces and then sewed it all back together again into a quilt. Sometimes I was sure she loved work.

These cars were not made to hold heat in for any length of time and certainly they didn't hold the cold out. By now I wished I had gone somewhere inside where it was warm, but there I sat in the back seat of the car stamping my feet to keep them warm and watched the few people walking up or down on the street. A door opened a short distance down the street and a man looked out and then looked up and down the street as if to see if all was clear. He re-entered and then directly backed out carrying one end of a table. The table had a heavy green throw draped over it, the kind a lot of people threw over their pianos in those days to keep the dust out. When the first man took a step backward, and down onto the sidewalk ....just for a moment the throw shifted and I could see two dangling arms and feet hanging down, from under the table. There was a man tied up under the table and that was why they had a throw on while they moved it.

The two men loaded it onto a truck that was sitting there and they drove off west over the bridge and out of sight. I had time to sit and ponder what I had seen and over my lifetime I have thought of this many times and have wondered just what was going on.

When my dad and mom came back to the car I was very excited and I tried to tell them what I saw. They thought I was telling them wild stories like I had been caught telling my grandpa and so they would not believe me.

You see my grand parents lived in one part of our old farm home and each night after the news was over on our battery powered radio I would go in and tell my grandpa the latest world news hot from the radio. I soon found out that the more exciting the news was the happier or more excited my grandfather seemed to get. I loved my grandfather dearly and I liked to see him happy so I poured it on. I would try to make it a bit more interesting for him.

You see my grandpa came from England and he longed for news of home so I tried to help him out if there was a bad fire in London and 6 people died I would make it an even dozen. If there was a wind storm in Liverpool, and took out a block of houses I would have it take out 3 blocks of houses. Grandpa got very excited which I thought was good. I was getting along just fine, or so I thought until my Grandfather started to ask my dad for more detail of these strange happenings. Oh boy! I was caught in what they called a lie.

This made everyone very sad and I was asked to explain what was going on. I said, "Well I found out that I could make my grandpa real happy by telling him large stories and the larger the story the more excited or happy grandpa got, and I thought that was good."

Dad and Mom were really provoked with me and they explained to me that this was just like lying. I promised them I would never to do this again not even to make my grandpa happy. I wondered if they would ever trust me again after what I had done?

I was never able to make my dad or mom believe the story of what I saw while sitting in the car, but to this day I swear it is true.

This was a lesson for me and I could see that when people know you tell lies they wont believe you when you tell the truth ... a lesson learned.

Many times when I drive through St.Marys I cannot help but wonder. What did I see?

The First TV Set

In 1951

TELEVISION

One morning in the winter of 1951 my sister Laurine's husband Oliver McIntosh came to visit us right after breakfast. He wanted us to go to his place to help him raise an aerial for his new television. Now until that moment, right then, I had not even heard of a television. I had no idea what it was. I realize today this sounds like a dumb question but is all truths I had to ask, "What is a television?" He tried to explain it to me. He said he had this square box with a screen on it, which would sit in the living room, and then there was an aerial sitting atop these water pipes he had welded together. This aerial was a bunch of rods and would pick up the picture and sort of throw it down some wires into the box and then we all could see the picture on the screen, just like a movie. He said all this with a very straight face.

Well now I didn't believe in magic, and it's hard enough at times to believe in God. I found it hard to believe my brother in law would spend his money on such a wild idea as this. Well we had to humour him, so dad and I went down to where he and Laurine first lived in a little house across the road from the old McIntosh homestead.

Oliver had welded several old water pipes together and they were lying on the ground on the north side of the house. The foot of the pipe was against the house foundation and the top straight out to the north.

He had the aerial fastened on the top of the pole and off the ground by putting it in his trailer box. One wire went over the back kitchen and was attached to his tractor tow bar. What he wanted dad and me to do was keep a wire tight on either side of the pipe as it went up so it would not jackknife one way or the other and come crashing down. All went well and some how we fastened the pipe to the side of the house and then several guy wires were fastened to iron stakes in the ground.

Now was time for the hour of truth. We all went into the house and sat in front of the box. When they turned it on, it went crazy, with lines going up on the screen, then down on the screen. Then with some skilful adjustment he made it look like snow. Other times the lines crossed the screen every which way, and yet another.

See, I knew the stupid thing would not work. Dad and I left in disgust and went home and started our now late morning barn chores. Technical Oliver was always years ahead of the rest of us but this time I was sure he had outdone himself, so I could not help but chuckle. He was going to be a long time living this one down.

About an hour later Laurine phone to tell us they now had a picture. Their Television set was an Admiral. I am not sure of the size but I think fourteen inches and they loved to watch Hockey Night In Canada and I love Lucy shows. This was the very first television I ever saw. It was hard to believe.

Some time after that my neighbours Ed and Joy Smith received their first T V set from their son Ralph who was now teaching school. He gave it to them no doubt in appreciation for the cost of putting him through school so he could be a teacher.

I often went to visit them in the evening. It was better than the movies as you not only saw a good movie, you had great company to share it with and lots of free coffee and food.

Joy earned a little pin money on the side by cutting the neighbour men's hair. She charged about fifty cents a haircut. Getting your hair cut was really a nice social evening. It included the haircut and a movie along with coffee and lunch. Now that is pretty good and all for fifty cents. After a hair cut one evening Ed and I were sitting watching T V with our feet up on the oven door of the kitchen stove. With a cup of coffee in hand we were absorbed in a good movie and I think happy in each other's company, when Joy suddenly said, "I smell smoke" The wood kindling was in the oven drying for the morning fire. It was smouldered and ready to burst into flame and as our feet were resting on it, our socks were scorching and smelling. Joy laughed and laughed and said, "You two would just sit there and catch fire if I didn't come and rescue you"

Dad and His Toys

My Dad and His Toys

Dad's 10 – 20 McCormick Deering Tractor

My dad loved machinery. While be was not the greatest mechanic, he was what I would say machinery minded. That is he understood belts and pulleys and cogs and chains much better than he understood valves and cylinders and gears and pistons. Like so many other farmers he was self-taught. From those little things that sometimes go wrong he and others like him earned their badge of respect.

As a boy dad drove horses on horse drawn machinery just as his dad, my grandfather had. It seemed that all farmers were able to adjust a seed drill and keep the manure spreader running smoothly. However a new world was at their doorstep. While some were able, even eager to move on, others did not like the idea of change.

First came steam power that still fascinates us to this day. However it was slow and cumbersome so the average farmer who loved his horses didn't get involved.

In 1923 the International Harvester McCormick Deering introduced the 4 cylinder 10 – 20 tractor. It was on steel spoke wheels with a wide rim of great cleats on the rear wheels for traction. Its pulley was 15 ¼ inches X 8 ½ inches and it ran at 645 rpm. It was classified as tractor to pull a two-furrow plough. They put out a new version of this tractor every year from 1923 to 1940. The 10 - 20 suffered the same fate as cars, as production was halted in 1940 because of The Second World War.

Sometime in the mid or late 1920's my dad bought a 10 – 20 McCormick Deering Tractor. I cannot tell you if it was a new one or a second hand one. In my memory this tractor had always been there. Dad shortened the tongue on some of the horse drawn machinery and for many more years got his full value out of them. No doubt my grandfather looked on disapprovingly watching his machinery being altered to be used by this monster, "The Tractor". He would however be greatful that it eased his workload and time spent in the field. Grandpa himself had no desire to mount the tractor. In fact I think he was rather fearful of it, as he didn't understand it. So much like the many seniors we have today and their fear of the computer.

It was the tractor of course that led dad into the world of farm machinery. Who can own a tractor and not have the toys to go with it?

From 1921 to 1929 the Canadian economy was booming. It has often been referred to as, "The Roaring Twenties." The Toronto, Montreal and New York stock markets had increased 3 fold in that time. Likewise all farm products were selling at record prices. It was a good time to expand your holdings, to buy more land and stock and equipment and it seems almost everyone did.

In the fall of 1929 dad bought the neighbouring farm of 62 and ½ acre. It was always referred to as, "The Barr Farm" as they were the original owners. In their hearts I know my dad and mom wanted to move out of the big farmhouse away from the older folks so they could more or less feel they were on their very own.

The Barr Farm

However shortly after they bought it on Tuesday October the 29th. The New York Stock Market crashed followed closely by the Toronto and Montreal Markets. Almost overnight the world for many came crashing down and they entered into a whole decade of depression from 1929 to 1939. It is often referred to as The Dirty Thirties or again as The Great Depression.

The farmers watched the value of their entire products go into decline; their grain, beef and pork markets all descended rapidly. People who had spent lavishly on farmland and equipment and had gone into debt were in deep trouble

For this reason dad and mom decided to rent out the house on their new farm to help earn some cash to pay the mortgage. A friend of dads by the name of Jack Young, his wife and I believe 3 children moved into the neat limestone house.

In 1931 my mom gave birth to my sister Pearl on March the 15th and that was the summer my dad had polio. It was through the great care of nurse Margaret Nairn of Motherwell that dad started on a long, long road to recovery.

Now it is amazing that I remember this but I do. Jack Young had a son called Jack Jr. and he was my age. One day when dad went to the Barr farm for something he took me along. This was the first time I remember meeting Jack Young Jr. Dad told young Jack to take me to the barn and show me his new threshing machine. I remember going into the horse stable door and up a staircase and opening the door on my left and seeing this all steel threshing machine. I remember it had the words "White Threshing Co." painted on it.

The White Threshing Machine made in London Ontario

George White made threshing machines in London Ontario as far back as 1889 but it seems like every other make of threshing machine at that time they thought bigger was better. All machines in those early days were made of kiln dried hard wood. In 1923 George White came out with a mid size all steel threshing machine. It was a machine that most farm tractors at that time could run. It was also supposed to be priced so that the average farmer could afford to own his own.

For better or for worse my dad had gone ahead and bought a threshing machine.

The recession turned into a depression and it seems there was no way dad could hang onto the farm or the threshing machine so he sold the machine and Mr. Barr took the farm back. It was not a happy ending, I remember my mom crying as she wanted to move into that little house where they could be on their own.

Many years later when I had the barbershop here in London I found myself driving my dad down to Windsor to visit a cousin who was not very well. On the way down we talked of many things.

I mentioned that first machine to him and he said, "But Jack you could not remember that machine as you were too young?" I would be 4 years old but coming 5 that fall.

I told him I remember that a Jack Young (who was our neighbour Agnes Morrison's brother) rented the house and that they had a son my age who was called Jack Jr. and when he was visiting the farm young Jack took me up the barn stairs to see the machine. Then I told dad I remember he had two crops planted on the farm that year running from the barn to my grandpa's farm to the north. The front part of the land towards the Mitchell Road was in winter wheat and the back part was oats and barley. When it came time to thresh he set the threshing machine up on the line where the two crops, the wheat and the mix grain met. After the crop was threshed, he burnt the straw and people drove from miles around to see what was burning.

Dad said he could not believe it but it was exactly right.

For a number of years after he sold the machine dad hired the threshing done. First by Watt Murray just a few farms south down the road. I remember being old enough to be in the granary bins filling them up and seeing to it the pipe never blocked. Even then it seemed the dust bothered me. Watt though had ambitious ideas as he sold the farm to Ed Neeb and bought a partnership in the International Harvester McCormick Deering dealership in St Marys.

About 1943 my dad parted with the 10 – 20 McCormick Deering and bought a model L Case tractor. It was quite old, I think it was built sometime in the mid 1930 It was a big powerful brute of a tractor on steel wheels and very hard to manoeuvre. It had a tall steel stick hand clutch on which dad put a pipe to extend its height so I could start and stop it easier. He eventually cut the wheels and fitted it with rubber tires. With no muffler on, its powerful engine barked out with a deafening sound that was very damaging to the ears.

Dad's Model L Case Tractor

Wes Parson of Munro did farm barn threshings for miles and miles around the country. He was a great guy and for many years Wes did the barn threshing for us and for many of our neighbours. It seems in those days there were always some men who specialized in odd jobs and over the years they got known for miles around as a good man to deal with.

One other such man that comes to mind was Jim Sidwell of Fullarton. If a storm blew off some barn shingles you called Jim. If you needed new back steps you called Jim. The good thing about it was you enjoyed having him work for you, as he was indeed "company." You knew he would do an excellent job and the price was always going to be right. Everyone liked Jim Sidwell and everyone liked John Wesley Parson better know as "Wes." Wes lived on a 50 acre farm on the south half of Lot 1, Con. 6 Hibbert Township, which is on the Fullarton Hibbert boundary. Besides threshing he did carpentry work and put in many land drains dug by hand the old fashioned way. Sometimes he hired a neighbour lad to help like my cousin Ivan Norris. Ivan was small but mighty and was always good for a few blisters.

But now back to threshing, -

By now I was old enough to go to barn threshings and do, as they would say, a man's work. It took about 6 to 8 men to form a threshing crew, and if you count the owner of the machine and the person in the granary and the man on the straw stack there would be closer to a dozen at the dinner table. In order to have free labour and afford to have your threshing done dad would send me out to 6 to 8 neighbourhood barn threshings and those farmers all had to send a man <u>as good as me</u> back to dad. Naturally having to send a man back <u>as good as me</u> presented quite a problem. Well not really as every one of our neighbours always gave us their best. That was the way we were with each other; no one was keeping count.

We enjoyed those years having Wes do the threshing. However there was a problem. It seemed that Wes' fame as a good man spread afar and the crops were good; thus it was late fall when the machine finally got to our place. Often it was cold even inside the barn and you were glad to work hard to keep warm.

Dad however never lost interest in owning his very own threshing machine. One day late in the fall I came home to find a huge old dull red wood machine sitting in the yard. I was rather shocked as it was so huge and looked so ancient. I hate to say this but to me it looked like a pile of junk. Dad assured me though it was a fine old threshing machine. All it needed was a bit of work. Little did I know that he had included me in that work?

The Goodison Thrashing Machine   (made of hard wood) made in Sarnia Ontario

This machine was a Goodison made by John Goodison of Sarnia, but by the look of the age of the machine I doubted very much if the "John Goodison" was still alive. It was a very old, dull red machine and the body made of wood. I remember he bought it in very late fall or perhaps in the winter.

As I was a lot smaller than my dad I spent a lot of time inside that machine freezing to death every afternoon that winter after dinner and the chores were done. We had to take out sieves after sieves to be fixed and then make repair to the agitators deep in its bowels and then fit them back into place. You must realize we had no hydro so I had a flashlight and a coal oil lantern inside to warm my hands and to see what I was doing. At other places there were sliding doors on the side of the machine where dad could hold the lantern up to guide me. To make these repairs we had to do it all manually as we had no power drills. Also remember we are working with kiln dried hard wood so fastening anything to that kind of wood is not easy, but when it is done right it holds firmly. In my cold confined place inside the machine I learned a lot about the works inside of a threshing machine that winter.

Most people just get to see the outside of the machine, to see and smell the dust, to hear the roar and feel the vibration. On the outside they watch with awe at a series of flying belts and whirling pulleys.

Actually while it all looks complicated it is a series of knives in the feeder that first cut the band or twine on the sheaves and spreads the sheaf as it enters the machine. Then there are fans to blow over the agitators. The agitators are best described as metal fingers that toss the straw up into the air while the fan blows the stocks and chaff towards the back of the machine. The heavier grain falls down on the sieves below and ends up in an auger that pushes the grain out on the right side of the machine. A blower then blows the grain up a pipe and from there it runs down hill into your granary bins. The straw ends up at the rear of the machine where a great fan type blower sucks and blasts it out the blower pipe, high onto the straw stack.

Dad and his good neighbour Ed Smith and family got together and decided to be our own threshing gang and do our own threshing. As Dad owned the machine to this day I have no idea what kind of agreement they had other than that dad got to do his threshing first. I can tell you this no agreement was ever written down on paper. It was all done by word of mouth and a handshake.

Being able to do our threshing this way saved us a lot of time and money and work, as we no longer had to haul the sheaves into the barn and store them in the mow waiting a day to be threshed. We now threshed each load as it entered the barn. The oldest Smith boy Ralph was the first to use their team and wagon to draw loads of grain in from the field and feed it into the threshing machine. Later Ron the second boy took over the job. Ron was small but mighty. Ed, their dad did all the pitching for both wagons, the Smith and ours. I have many happy memories of those hours we spent together working under the sun. Things always go better when you work with true friends.

Dad looked after the machine and the running of the straw blower and watched the granary. Sometimes I thought he had the easy end of things, as certainly I know he enjoyed his part. I can picture him now running around with an oilcan or a can of grease in one hand and a shingle stick in the other to pack grease into the grease cups. He was always on the go. The old machine was covered with grease cups fittings to be filled with grease and oil openings to be kept lubricated with oil. The last thing you wanted to find was a hot bearing, as that would soon bring trouble. Actually the machine didn't give us a lot of trouble. I don't think we ever had a real break down over all the years we had the old machine. So I must have done a darn good job inside of it.

The thing that bothered me the most was getting it in or out of the barn. It was a monster on wheels made of hard wood and the insides were steel. Thankfully by now my dad had a much larger tractor, a model L Case to use on the machine. The threshing machine came with a heavy cable and several pulleys and 2 huge grab hooks.

I don't think dad understood the right way to hook the pulleys onto the beam to make it easier to draw it in. He did try it a few times but the great grab hook was damaging the beams in the barn so he gave that up. Dad put a long tongue on the front of the machine and pushed it in with the tractor. In the end he always succeeded but I was sure one of us would get killed one day. The machine would often jackknife onto the tractor. It would just toss the tractor aside like a toy. Dad would have us standing by the rear wheels of the threshing machine ready to block the wheel if it jackknifed and descended onto him. However sometimes it would jack knife and jump the blocks and attack the tractor. It was scary. Once the rear end of the machine was on the main barn floor heavy planks were put behind the wheels for it to roll onto, as we were afraid the machine's weight might take the floor down.

One year for some reason the Smiths decided to sit the machine on the ground outside the front of the barn but close enough so they could blow the straw inside. Dad or Ed was up a tall ladder prying off a long board on the end of the barn so they could put the straw blower in. At the same moment Ralph's mom Joy Smith arrived with lemonade. She had just handed me a glass and was pouring it full. I looked up and I saw the long hemlock board jump free from the barn and start to fall. I reached out and pushed Joy back as the board landed flat and at its exact center on the top of my head. There was a moment of silence I believe as everyone thought I would be hurt and they were looking for blood. However there I stood with a 12 or 14-foot board on my head with the ends flapping up and down gracefully. I on the other hand still had a full glass of lemonade. I didn't spill a drop. The Smith clan still chuckle about this incident today.

Barn threshing eventually came to an end as the combine invaded its territory and became more and more popular.

My dad bought a Forage Harvester for haying and this same outfit made it possible for him to pick up the straw in the field after it was combined. We often combined a field of wheat every fall. Many others were combining their whole crop and picking up the straw with a baler or harvester just like my dad's. So dad decided this was the way to go

Dad and His Forage Harvester and The John Deere Tractor

That was one thing that always bothered me. My dad never thought to ask what I thought of his idea. Dad had me unloading the wagonloads of hay or straw at the barn onto the blower where it was blown into the mow. That in itself was a hard and dusty job. I never had the pleasure of going to the field with the harvester.

So his threshing days ended when he sold the old machine and hired the crop combined. I was never totally happy about this though as it seems when you combine the chaff and the leafy part of the straw falls through the stubble onto the ground. The straw loses a lot of its value. It does not make nice soft bedding and the straw loses almost all of its food value.

I missed the old threshing machine for a long time, as it had become a part of the barn floor. It was also a treasured part of history that we find hard to forget. We are glad that we can say, "Been there and done that," as it is now all history.

One of my dad's best investments was a John Deere AR tractor. Like everything else he ever bought he never told me he was thinking of trading the Model L Case. I just came home one day and found the John Deere in the yard. I wasn't exactly happy as the John Deere was a 2-cylinder tractor and went putt putt - putt – putt. However after using it for awhile I learned to love it. He soon bought a smaller tractor for a second tractor for small jobs. It was an Allis Chalmers. Again I had no idea he was going to buy a small tractor until I saw it in the yard.

While dad was happy to let me drive his tractors ploughing his fields or pulling the disks or cultivators, thus eating a lot of great old farm dirt, he never allowed me to touch the threshing machine or the forage harvester itself.
These were his toys and I had to respect that.

The Country Garden

The Country Garden

Whether you lived in town or a village or on a farm everyone needed a garden. A garden on the farm held a very important place in those early years of our pioneer forefathers. The old style of mixed farming would never be complete unless it included a jewel of a garden. That garden was somewhere handy to the house, or let us say not a far walk from the kitchen door. It had a small gate to allow easy entrance and it was fenced on all four sides by a special kind of wire fence made to keep chickens and small animals out. This fencing had a narrow spacing of the wire at the bottom and the spacing grew wider as it ascended to the top.

For many, gardening was a natural. I suppose it was because by nature we were farmers, tillers of the soil and we had a yen to grow things. It just seemed natural that at least one person in every family excelled at gardening and became the family gardener. In our case, I got the job. I don't remember volunteering for the job but my sisters never tried to undo this or to take it from me. Somehow it was written down in the good book. "Jack was the gardener". I have never regretted the training I received from my grandparents or my mom both in the vegetable garden and the flowerbeds. I consider it the gift of a lifetime and over the years it has given me many hours of pleasure.

In those early years before his death in 1941 my Grandfather Cooke loved a good garden. He liked to grow a few things that they grew in his native England, things that my mom would not grow. The one I remember the most was called Broad Beans. I never really learned to like them but I ate them because my grandpa grew them. Anything my grandpa did had to be ok.

For others a garden may have represented work, but still they had a garden of sorts. If it wasn't done for the love of gardening then it was at least for the basic need of survival.

Over the winter and on into spring the vegetables in the family's cellar were gradually depleted. It got to the place one had to work hard to find the last few carrots buried deep in rich black earth in the wooden barrel. The winter-stored cabbages were long gone before spring and the turnip pit in the field was almost empty. The potatoes in the bin were getting soft as they did every spring, but we would still use them in hopes they would last until new potatoes arrived from the garden a few weeks down the road. Perhaps the last of the apples were left shrivelled in the almost empty apple bin. Somehow it seemed even when the apple bin looked hopeless mom would come up with yet one more bowl of her great homemade applesauce.

Keep in mind that the local country stores didn't sell vegetables and it might be 10 or more miles to the nearest town. So to harness old Daisy to the sleigh and drive into town for carrots was unheard of. Besides in winter the carrots would freeze on the way home.

Now just think of it, in those early years next to a cow for milk and the hens for eggs the old-fashioned country garden held the most honoured place of importance on a farm.

I think many of us can picture our mothers with a straw hat on, out in the garden picking beans or cutting lettuce for dinner. Somehow it was in harmony with the way we lived.

As we got older we were all introduced to the hoe and earned our veggies by the sweat on our brow and the blisters on our hands. Still if you were a gardener as I was, the garden was a place where everyday miracles took place. I watched the tiny seed sprout and turn into a leaf. I watched that leaf mature and grow into a plant and then in turn become an edible vegetable. Thus today I can recognize almost all vegetables and flowers by the seed, leaf, or plant. I don't have to wait to know if it's a radish or a cucumber.

There were times when I was troubled perhaps by the thing I had or had not done and the garden would be a place of quiet refuge, a place where you could retreat for quiet times and to think. Believe me, being the only boy in the family; I had to do that a lot.

It was also a great place to learn all about nature, worms and bugs in which I took great interest and delight. Have you ever seen those great big juicy green, yellow and black tomato worms with evil looking horns? I would knock them from the plant into a tin can. Many times I chased my sisters out of the garden with a handsome tomato worm just to hear them scream. Some years there were hordes of potato bugs or green cabbageworms to deal with. Then there were scarecrows to build and dress to keep the birds from pulling up the corn. Every now and then a small rabbit came in under the fence and had to be chased out by the dog. Life was never dull around a good garden.

Those early gardens were well fenced so as to keep the hens or a wandering cow out. The garden was ploughed with a single furrow, hand held, horse pulled plough, and worked with a horse drawn cultivator. My mom never seemed to believe in straight rows. Thus many foreign words were exchanged between my dad and Frank the old horse that was used for such work. Old Frank had seen better days and by now had it figured he had already earned his oats. He was tired and perhaps just a wee bit lazy. It seems in his old age Frank could not walk a straight line. He was more like a drunken sailor. Mom's row drifted south and old Frank drifted north and poor dad tried to cultivate the area between.

Eventually the horses became old-fashioned or outdated for the job but the tractors often could not manoeuvre within the fenced area of the enclosed garden. Thus in time the gardens were placed out in the field somewhere close to the house. Perhaps being placed out there it lost its country charm. Still we had everything from loads of pumpkins to watermelons and those strange citrons that looked like watermelons my mom used to insist on growing. Mom would take the outside rind off just as you would a pumpkin and then take the seed out as you would a watermelon. After cutting it into small square bits she cooked it, making it into fruit that I never learned to like.

As children we would play with a citron all winter long on the old kitchen floor. We would sit on the floor with our legs spread apart and roll the citron back and forth to each other. As it neared spring, much to out despair mom would ask us to give it up as it was needed as food for the table. It was like eating an old friend. I didn't enjoy it at all.

Potatoes were planted in the garden very early in the spring for summer use on the kitchen table. There is nothing like having your very own early potatoes for dinner. The main lot of potatoes however were grown out in the field. These were planted later so they could be harvested in cool weather late in the fall. That way they would keep solid in the cool cellar all winter.

Mom would start her garden plants from seed very early somewhere between late winter or very early spring. I could never get used to growing tomatoes and cabbages on the windowsill. I simply hated seeing it done and I still do today. On cold nights mom would put some newspaper between the pane and the plants to be sure they didn't get frost. It was nothing to see the kitchen windows all frosted up in the morning.

How it would work out had a lot to do with the timing of your planting and who knows when old man winter decides to go and spring arrives. If you plant your seeds too soon your plants will end up tall and flimsy. The neighbours all watched each other's plants grow and it made for good table talk with the coffee. "How are your tomatoes doing"?

When mom planted her tomatoes she always had her cedar shingles ready. Two shingles were used for each plant. The tomato plant or cabbage was planted in the centre of a shallow hole and two shingles set into the ground sheltering the plants from the wind or the hot sun. For a few days water was poured in the low area around the plant. As the plant grew the low area was filled in with earth giving the plant a stronger stock.

It was many years later that those wire cages were invented to hold tomato plants upright. At that time everyone used wooden stakes and tied the plant to the stake with a strip of cloth. Everyone knew what you meant when you said you staked your tomatoes today.

In those early years we didn't seem to have as many problems growing things as they have today. I guess you would say almost all of our fruit and vegetables would be classified today as organic grown. Gardening, whether it is a flower garden or a vegetable garden is a part of our heritage. Something passed on from one generation to another? I would like to even cherished classify it as an art. I fear we have lost something that was once a part of ...the way we lived.

Will You Remember Me Jack-A

Will You Remember Me Jack-A

On his dying bed I remember his words and my promise.

Every day I rushed home from public school to my grandfather's bedside fearful of what I might find. It was April of 1941 and my Grandpa Cooke was dying of cancer. I was 12 years old and I am not sure that I yet fathomed the finality of death. For weeks we had watched grandpa lie there and deteriorate. He had never been a big man and because of a lifetime of hard work on the farm he always remained lean. The cancer was now well advanced and he had not been able to eat any solid food for some time. He could however swallow a small amount of liquid. He was not a drinking man but the doctor had recommended that he drink brandy.

It is known that in the old days when you were sick the doctors often recommended brandy for comfort. The story goes that you should hang your hat on the wall and go to bed and drink brandy until you saw two hats. However my grandmother looked after the bottle and doled it out in a small shot glass, so my grandpa never got to see two hats.

I had spent a lot of time in my childhood with my grandpa. It seemed I found in him what I couldn't find in my dad, someone I could share time with, to ask questions of, and always get a straight answer. At 12 years of age I knew I loved my grandpa dearly and I knew without a doubt he loved me too. Of course there was my grandma too, I loved her but I had this special bond with my grandpa.

I still remember that day I made the promise. I can see him lying there on his back in bed in the darkened bedroom looking very frail and weak. His life was slowly ebbing from him day by day, hour by hour.

I had arrived home from school and as always he was happy to see me. I am sure he was awaiting my arrival. After a few moments of silence he looked at me very seriously and said, "Jack-A, will you remember me?" (my grandpa always called me Jack-A, not Jackie)

In my heart I knew it was more a plea than a question. I had been made well aware he was dying. I knew he wondered if after he was gone, in time would I forget him. Would his life be remembered for who he was or would it disappear as ashes in the wind? Would I remember him as the grandfather he had tried so hard to be?

I was only twelve years old but I looked him in the face and solemnly made the promise.

"I will never, never, forget you grandpa."
Grandpa died April 21st.1941.

Those of you who have read my books will know I kept my promise to remember him.

Every year about June I find myself driving up to St. Marys and with my sister Laurine. We drive out to the old St Marys Cemetery to tend my grandparent's gravestone. We scrub it clean of a red fungus that covers many of the gravestones in that cemetery.

It is then I remember my promise and there is a feeling of comfort in a promise kept.

Epilogue

*"Ain't it fine
when things are going
Topsy-turvy and askew,
To discover someone showing
Good old-fashioned faith in you?
Ain't it good when life
seems dreary
And your hopes about to end,
Just to feel the handclasp cheery
Of a fine old loyal friend?"*

Edgar Guest

Epilogue

Have you ever noticed that a little encouragement can go a long ways towards setting you on the path to achieve many things, both big and small? Perhaps even things you may have never attempted to do otherwise. Yes, even those things you may have thought far beyond the realm of your thoughts or skill.

I think we all have certain talents that the good Lord has given to us. Sometimes these talents are all but hidden from us. That is, we take them for granted, as they are just our everyday things, our ideas and thoughts and our ways of doing things. Others though, sometimes see what we don't see in ourselves and that is our talent and our skills. I have often watched my brother-in-law Bill Butler work with tools in his workshop and I have wished many times I had his skill. Yet I believe Bill goes about making things and fixing things everyday with little thought about the skill he has in those two hands.

So never underestimate yourself, take pride in what you do and don't give up. I was sure my first book; "Getting By In A Silent World" was a one-time thing.

"Not so," said Ralph and Eleanor Smith of Goderich, two retired schoolteachers who constantly urged me to write again. They claim they enjoy reading my writing but could it be because of their great need to check over someone's homework? So a special thank you Ralph and Eleanor for your encouragement and faith in me.

I also want to thank my friend Don Peever of London who tirelessly taught me so much about the computer. This time I was able to handle the pictures for the book myself except for the cover and that great skill was the work of Don Peever

While most of the pictures in my book are my own I would like to thank my friend Bill Stephens for the use of his fine old photos of horses working in the field. They bring back priceless memories of an era long past. .

It has been a busy spring and summer for me looking after flower gardens and huge pots for the condo property along with my own on my balcony. Then I have two other flower gardens here that I look after daily, belonging to neighbours who are not well.

Usually when I am at work at the front of the building some of the neighbours drop by, so often being towed by four legged critters, both large and small. The dogs themselves know me well and express their joy at seeing me once more. I expect it is because of my earthy scents that they approve of me so much. Thus far I have managed to keep my pant legs dry. Since spring these neighbours have followed the garden's growth daily and they express their delight at watching the flower garden explode into multi-colour from the

8 inch Portulaca to the 5 foot Cannas. It is in their ooohs and ahhhs that I reap satisfaction and a just reward.

However the season is moving on and already my flower gardens are showing signs of maturity. Indeed it is a reminder of fall. Still they, like you and me, linger on with the hope that life is not all over just because of our fading bloom.

I am not really a summer person as what summer heat does to the air cuts down on my breathing. Thus I must pick the day or time-o-day to go about. So I look forward to the fall with its cooler air and its enchanting colours. No doubt I will be out there with my camera in hand, venturing out of town and even back to my home country. There I will roam my old rural haunts in search of just the right picture - a picture that perhaps will remind me of yet other stories of those yester-years.

Winter does not present a problem for me as it seems people slow down and that allows me to catch up. Instead of rambling hither and yonder they hibernate.

I hope every one of you can find a memory … a little of yourself, in each of the stories in my book. Looking back we realize we have had the better of two worlds. While we enjoy what we have today, we still feel enriched by our past.

I am sure there have been many times that a seed was planted in your thoughts by someone and you have said, "That reminds me of the time" and that is how I was able to write this book. Inside each of you there is a story waiting to be told.

Hope You Have Had a Happy Read ……… Jack

www.ingramcontent.com/pod-product-compliance
Lightning Source LLC
Chambersburg PA
CBHW062126160426
43191CB00013B/2208